BLUEPRINTS

Physical Education
Key Stage 1

Win Heath

Cecilia Gregory

Julie Money

Gavin Peat

Judy Smith

Gareth Stratton

Stanley Thornes (Publishers) Ltd

BLUEPRINTS – HOW TO GET MORE INFORMATION

Blueprints is an expanding series of practical teacher's ideas books and photocopiable resources for use in primary schools. Books are available for every Key Stage of every core and foundation subject, as well as for an ever-widening range of other primary needs. **Blueprints** are carefully structured around the demands of the National Curriculum but may be used successfully by schools and teachers not following the National Curriculum in England and Wales.

Blueprints provide:

- Total National Curriculum coverage
- Hundreds of practical ideas
- Books specifically for the Key Stage you teach
- Flexible resources for the whole school or for individual teachers
- Excellent photocopiable sheets – ideal for assessment, SATs and children's work profiles
- Supreme value.

Books may be bought by credit card over the telephone and information obtained on (0242) 228888. Alternatively, photocopy and return this FREEPOST form to join our mailing list. We will mail you regularly with information on new and existing titles.

Please add my name to the BLUEPRINTS mailing list. *Photocopiable*

Name _____

Address_____

_____

_____

Postcode_____

To: Marketing Services Dept., Stanley Thornes Publishers, FREEPOST (GR 782), Cheltenham, Glos. GL53 1BR

First published in 1994 by:
Stanley Thornes (Publishers) Ltd
Ellenborough House
Wellington Street
CHELTENHAM GL50 1YD

A catalogue record for this book is available from the British Library.

ISBN 0–7487–1639–4

Typeset by Tech-Set, Gateshead, Tyne & Wear
Printed and bound in Great Britain at the Bath Press, Avon.

CONTENTS

INTRODUCTION

What is *Blueprints Physical Education?*

Blueprints Physical Education is a practical classroom resource written to fulfil all the requirements of the National Curriculum for physical education at primary school level. It is intended to be used flexibly, either as an ideas bank for individual teachers or as a workable core resource for a whole school's scheme of work in physical education.

Blueprints Physical Education consists of a teacher's resource book for each of the primary key stages. Together they provide a coherent spiral curriculum for primary physical education.

Blueprints Physical Education and the National Curriculum

Physical Education is a foundation subject within the National Curriculum. It comprises six areas of activity outlined in the Key Stage 1: Programme of Study (activity specific):

Athletic activities
Dance
Games
Gymnastic activities
Outdoor and Adventurous activities
Swimming.

This book covers five of the six areas. As swimming is a continuum of learning that cannot be easily broken up by key stage, it has been decided to treat it entirely in *Blueprints Physical Education Key Stage 2*.

You will also find that games and athletics have been combined into one section in this book, as they can be most effectively managed together in classroom planning. This book is therefore divided into four main sections:

Dance
Gymnastics
Games and Athletics
Outdoor and Adventurous Activities.

The book aims to provide you with a complete scheme of work for Key Stage 1 Physical Education. This is provided by units of work which give you outline lesson plans and by an activities bank for each area of physical education. There is also a bank of core movement skills which are widely used in primary PE.

You will find that the material is structured so that there is progression from Reception/Year 1 through to Year 2. Reception/Year 1 have been planned jointly as in the majority of schools these pupils carry out their physical education programme together.

For each area of activity you will find a structured bank of materials, comprising the following:

About the area of activity: an introduction giving you essential information about the area of physical education being covered.

National Curriculum requirements at Key Stage 1: this reproduces the content of your National Curriculum ringbinder exactly and provides an at-a-glance guide to the coverage of that particular area of activity.

Teaching the area of activity at Key Stage 1: this provides you with a clear strategy for breaking down and tackling the area of physical education in the classroom into key themes which provide the bases for the units of work which follow. It gives you important teaching points to watch out for in teaching the area of PE. You will also find that it provides you with model lessons which take examples from the lesson plans that follow and explain in detail teaching strategies for teaching that area of PE. In each model lesson the three processes are identified by:

PL – Plan
P – Perform
EV – Evaluate.

The three strands are identified by:

! – Safety
WWO – Working with others
H – Health related fitness.

Cross-curricular links are identified by an X.

Activity bank: there is a bank of activities for each area of PE. These provide progressive activities basic to each area. You will find these continuously referred to in the lesson plans.

Lesson plans: these are provided for Reception/Year 1 and Year 2. They provide you with a complete outline scheme of work for physical education. As you will see, each lesson plan has the same structure in terms of Introduction, Development and Conclusion. This layout ensures a sound progression of the theme throughout the lesson. The lesson plans are sometimes divided into units of work.

A time allocation has been made for each area of activity based on a realistic assessment of time available and needs for physical education, as follows:

	Reception/Year 1	Year 2
Gymnastics	18 lessons	18 lessons
Dance	18 lessons	18 lessons
Games/Athletics	27 lessons	27 lessons
Outdoor/Adventurous Activities	18 lessons	18 lessons

The way in which these are planned into your school timetable will depend on the facilities and equipment. It is important that you do provide the opportunity for all of your children to have the experience of the activities as identified in the National Curriculum at Key Stage 1. These activities provide a foundation of skills essential for children to learn if they are going to progress at Key Stage 2 and develop their knowledge, understanding and skill. They provide the basic introduction to opportunities for physical education, sport and dance for life. You will find a year planner suggesting how you might organise PE on page vi.

PE at Key Stage 1 ▷

If children are to develop a wide and full repertoire of skills then the earlier they are given the appropriate learning experiences the better. It is therefore necessary that you as the teacher give them the opportunity to discover and understand what their bodies can do through the activities presented in this book. At this age the children are physically active and 'hungry' to improve and extend their potential in a wide movement context. Each child can gain not only from developing their skill level but from the quality of experience that you can offer them. So that this quality of experience is clearly identified, teachers should be aware of the stages of development of the children so that the selection of work is appropriate to their ability and progress. The end of key stage statements and Programme of Study (General) clearly state the knowledge and understanding children should have acquired by the end of Key Stage 1.

> It is the sum total of all the end key stage statements and requires pupils to demonstrate knowledge, skill and understanding involved in the process of planning, performing and evaluating physical activities; and in aspects of health related exercise. (NC 1992, B2)

PE gives each child the opportunity to discover what the body is capable of doing in a variety of situations and the control needed to achieve actions in a variety of physical activities. PE provides activity which is enjoyable and worthwhile and essential for the development of a healthy body and mind. Through being physically active it allows the children to develop a good self-image and gives them the opportunity to communicate and co-operate with others.

The quality of experience presented to your children will be affected by planning and preparation and how you transmit this planning into the activities. This book is designed so that these matters can be addressed effectively by you.

At this age the selection of material and appropriateness of the level of task can vary according to the stage of development. For example, initially you would have the children working individually, progressing to pair work and by the end of Key Stage 1 to small group work. Different tasks and the use of space will also change as the children progress through this key stage so that they have to learn to adjust to different demands. Also they need to experience a variety of equipment. For example in the early stages of throwing and catching, children should have the experience of handling balls of different sizes and shapes – a large, slow-moving ball would be most beneficial to begin with, ultimately progressing to a small, quick-moving ball. This development can only be successful if the lessons have been carefully planned and structured, and properly resourced.

Children at Key Stage 1 need to experiment and have a width of movement experience presented to them. The term movement is central to all areas of PE. For example, in gymnastics it is the management of the body in relation to the task that is important, whilst in dance the movement is used expressively. In games it is how the body uses and controls the apparatus. The action of the body is therefore a primary concern in all activities, in particular when apparatus is being used or when two or more children are playing together in a game situation.

Movement is often referred to as the

What
Where } these are identified in the programme of study (activity specific)
How

What: focuses on particular parts of the body. For example, ball skills – using hands/feet; travelling, sending and receiving.

Where: space in which the children move. This can be their own space, or shared with others. For example, travel in different directions; show two shapes using a low and high level.

How: does the body move through a variety of actions? For example, throwing a ball; dynamics in dance. Here the elements of how the body moves are related to the use of weight, space, time and flow.

There is a core of basic movement skills that underly all PE learning at Key Stage 1 and which are continuously called upon in this book. You will find these set out on pages 5–7. It will help if you are closely familiar with the development of the core skills.

Managing PE at Key Stage 1 ▷

If children are to be offered the full range of activities as identified in the National Curriculum, then the programme for PE at Key Stage 1 needs to be clearly organised and managed. Many schools do have a member of staff in charge of the subject – a curriculum leader whose responsibility is to promote and develop the subject in the school. The curriculum leader will offer help and support for other colleagues, be able to take on a leadership role in planning, teaching and evaluating the PE programme, and give advice on implementing the NC. If PE is to be fully recognised by all teachers then the curriculum leader has a major role to play in promoting PE and developing confidence amongst inexperienced teachers or those teachers who feel ill equipped or even dislike teaching the subject.

The success of any subject is dependent upon the human and facility resources available and their effective and efficient deployment. In *Blueprints Physical Education Key Stage 2* there is a section that provides a model for managing opportunities for physical education not only in the primary school but in the school's community.

If the National Curriculum is to be fulfilled then teachers need to re-evaluate the potential of the following essential areas:

Equipment: There needs to be a variety of equipment so that children have the experience of handling different sizes/weights as they progress through Key Stage 1.

Working areas: Outside facilities should be used for games/athletics. The playground needs to have a sound and safe surface so that, for example, balls are not hindered by holes which may make the balls rise. If there are playing fields then these need to be flat, well cut and drained and free from debris.

Hall: This area will be used by different activities in your school. It is therefore important that when dance/gymnastics are taking place the floor is clean and equipment is safely placed at the side of the hall. When the pupils are working in the hall, bare feet should be encouraged. This helps the children to strengthen their feet, but more importantly they are able to be aware of how they use their feet.

Below is a possible way of presenting a PE timetable over the two years. This two-year planner has been designed with the assumption that there are three lessons per week for PE. Taken into account is Term 2 when the weather makes it difficult to go outside and the hall space is only available for one PE lesson. This year planner has been designed to support the assessment which emphasises the whole curriculum process.

Activity	Term 1	Term 2	Term 3
Gym	Weeks 1–9		Weeks 1–9
Dance	Weeks 1–9	Weeks 1–9	
Games and Athletics	Weeks 1–9	Weeks 1–9	Weeks 1–9
Outdoor and Adventurous Activities		Weeks 1–9	Weeks 1–9

Activity	Term 4	Term 5	Term 6
Gym	Weeks 1–9	Weeks 1–9	
Dance		Weeks 1–9	Weeks 1–9
Games and Athletics	Weeks 1–9	Weeks 1–9	Weeks 1–9
Outdoor and Adventurous Activities	Weeks 1–6	Weeks 1–6	Weeks 1–6

Observation and assessment

Observation and assessment are essential for you to improve your curriculum planning, evaluate your teaching and review your objectives. Observation of your children enables you to facilitate their learning experiences within each activity and this is linked to assessment. The end of key stage statements provide the necessary framework for assessing the children and planning the next stages of learning. The key area to observe is the evidence of performance within all activities; it is important to give the children the opportunity to discuss and describe their own work and that of others in the class. Assessment of the children's work should be continuous throughout the activities and not just at the end of the key stage.

The keeping of records should not be too demanding at this key stage but some evidence of how the child is progressing should be available to child, teacher and parent. If this information is recorded the teacher will be able to establish what the child knows, understands and can achieve. As well as monitoring the level of achievement, the child's effort and involvement need to be taken into account. For this reason we have provided some recording sheets (on pages vii–viii) which you may like to use.

During Key Stage 1 the following areas should be assessed through observation:

- Observation – reporting verbally their own movement or that of others.
- Understanding – being able to plan and evaluate movement within the required task.
- Safety – being aware of their own personal safety and that of others in the various activities. Knowing the importance of safety procedures in moving equipment.
- Health – understanding the importance of effects of physical activity on the body and aspects such as cleanliness and changing for PE.
- Working with others – having the ability to co-operate.
- Attitude – showing a positive attitude to all physical activity.

This is not intended as a checklist but as a focus for your own personal observation of how your children are progressing. This follows the process model of watching the pupil in planning, performing and evaluating the various activities. In some instances information will be gathered by discussing with pupils during and after lessons to monitor their level of understanding. In order to help you collect relevant evidence related to a set task, we have provided two record sheets:

- Record Sheet 1: this could be used for each term or in conjunction with the year planner. It will enable you to collect ongoing evidence to assess pupils' progress and facilitate the achievement of end of key stage statements. Each box should be completed with a grade: good/satisfactory/weak. Good means that the pupil is competent at this end of key stage statement in this particular activity. Satisfactory means that the pupil can achieve but lacks flair and the ability to adapt to different situations. Weak means that the pupil lacks the ability to put into practice the required end of key stage statements.
- Record sheet 2: This can provide an assessment for the end of Key Stage 1. The above grading method could also be used.

Record sheet 1

Name:	Date:
Key Stage:	Term:

Programme of study (general)

Pupils should be able to:	Gymnastics	Dance	Games/ Athletics	Outdoor and Adventurous Activities
1) perform a wide range of simple movements in a variety of activities with and without equipment				
2) recognise and make up simple rules, and work within them				
3) use movement and show moods and feelings and respond to simple rhythms and contrasting stimuli				
4) link movements with increasing control to show changes of direction or level and variations of speed, tension or rhythm.				
5) recognise and follow safety procedures, including lifting, carrying and moving equipment				
6) practise and perform simple skills				
7) improve performance when working alone and, when ready, in co-operation with a partner				
8) describe own and other's achievements in physical education, and how they did it, using simple, functional and aesthetic terms				
9) describe changes that happen to own body during exercise				

Observation and comments to support achievement as the pupil progresses through Key Stage 1 with particular reference to Programmes of Study (activity specific)

Record sheet 2

Assessment at the end of Key Stage 1 Name:			Date:	
By the end of the key stage pupils should be able to:	Gymnastics	Dance	Games/ Athletics	Outdoor and Adventurous Activities
a) plan and perform safely a range of simple actions and linked movements in response to given tasks and stimuli				
b) practise and improve their performance				
c) describe what they and others are doing				
d) recognise the effects of physical activity on their bodies				

Observation and comments based on individual achievement at Key Stage 1

GUIDE TO PE IN THE NATIONAL CURRICULUM

The National Curriculum for Physical Education is a single attainment target. This encompasses all the end of key stage statements which incorporate the processes of planning, performing and evaluating. Throughout the document the focus is on activity and performance. The programmes of study provide the teacher with a planning base plus information about how the skills and processes will enable children to achieve the Attainment Target as defined by the end of key stage statements.

There are three parts identified in the programmes of study:

• General requirements which should apply to all key stages and be taught through all areas of activity.
• General programmes of study which are identified for each key stage and must be taught through all the areas of activity for the key stage to meet the objectives as presented in the end of key stage statements.
• Activity specific programmes of study which refer to each area of activity at each key stage (athletic activities, dance, gymnastic activities, outdoor and adventurous activities and swimming).

You will find all the requirements set out below. You will also find that the activity specific programmes of study are set out at the front of each area of activity.

General requirements
Physical education involves pupils in the continuous process of planning, performing and evaluating. These general requirements supplement both the general and activity specific programmes of study for each key stage. The general requirements reflect good practice so they need to be at the forefront of planning lessons.

General programmes of study
These are taught in all the activities and represent the process involved in planning, performing and evaluating. It is necessary that the children are involved in PE lessons and that they are guided through a process of learning and that you as the teacher create opportunities for the children to plan their involvement in the lesson, to practise their ideas and, most importantly, to evaluate how effective their ideas have been. The children also need time to reflect on and refine their actions so that they can see the benefits of the process model.

Activity specific programmes of study
These provide the content of PE and are the areas which will provide the framework when planning the PE programme.

Highlighted in the Non-Statutory Guidance of the National Curriculum are the following Cross-Curricular elements:

Health
Safety
Personal and social skills.

Health
Each activity plays a part in promoting a sound and healthy attitude to PE. The end of key stage statements and programme of study (general) provide a framework for relating how exercise affects the body. This is where you as the teacher should make sure that each lesson involves the children in activities which use whole body movements. The children need to understand the importance of changing for PE lessons and develop a positive awareness of hygiene principles as well as establishing good habits in how they use their bodies and adopting good posture.

Safety
In the programmes of study particular attention is drawn to the area of safety. It is your responsibility as the teacher to make sure that the environment is a safe place to work in and that the children are appropriately dressed for the activity and are able to move freely. All jewellery needs to be removed so that there is no danger of catching or damaging themselves or others.

It is important that the children learn to handle equipment safely when lifting, carrying and placing. Children should be made aware of their own safety and that of others in all the activities, and should readily respond to your instructions and signals. It is necessary at this age that routines are established in terms of codes of practice and rules. If these habits are formed early in the children's PE activities then they will gain the benefit of a life-long attitude to safety.

Personal and social skills
From Key Stage 1, PE needs to promote children's understanding of how to present themselves in a co-operative manner when working individually or as a group. They must be allowed the opportunity to understand themselves and the attributes and capabilities they possess. Children also need time to practise social skills through different strategies in terms of teaching and learning styles.

All PE activities should promote equal opportunities. The PE curriculum should give all children the opportunity to develop their full potential in a balanced curriculum. Individual needs, abilities and interests should be catered for through a well-planned and progressive programme. If this is the case, then the children will develop enjoyment and satisfaction from planning, performing and evaluating a balanced range of movement activities.

1

General requirements relating to programmes of study: requirements for all key stages

Physical education involves pupils in the continuous process of planning, performing and evaluating. The following requirements should apply to all key stages and be taught through all areas of activity. They supplement both the general and area specific programmes of study for each key stage.

In physical education lessons pupils should be taught to:
- be physically active;
- demonstrate knowledge and understanding mainly through physical actions rather than verbal explanations;
- be aware at the same time of terminology relevant to activities undertaken; and
- engage in activities that involve the whole body, maintain flexibility and develop strength and endurance.

In order to become independent learners pupils should be enabled to:
- solve for themselves the problems that they will encounter in the course of their physical activities;
- evaluate initial attempts and decide how to modify subsequent attempts; and
- consolidate particular skills through practice and repetition.

In order to develop positive attitudes pupils should be encouraged to:
- observe the conventions of fair play, honest competition and good sporting behaviour;
- understand and cope with a variety of outcomes, including both success and failure;
- be aware of the effects and consequences of their actions on others and on the environment; and
- appreciate the strengths and be aware of the weaknesses of both themselves and others in relation to different activities.

To ensure safe practice pupils should be taught to:
- be concerned with their own and others' safety in all activities undertaken;
- understand the importance of warming up for, and recovery from, exercise, thus preventing injury;
- adopt good posture and the correct use of the body at all times;
- lift, carry and place equipment safely;
- observe the rules of good hygiene;
- understand why particular clothing, footwear and protection are worn for different activities;
- understand the safety risks of wearing inappropriate clothing, footwear and jewellery; and
- respond readily to instructions and signals within established routines and follow relevant rules and codes.

Key stage 1: Programmes of study (activity specific)

At key stage 1, pupils should pursue the programmes of study for five areas of activity: athletic activities, dance, games, gymnastic activities, outdoor and adventurous activities, and if the school chooses to teach it in key stage 1, swimming.

Athletic Activities	Dance	Games	Gymnastic activities	Outdoor & adventurous activities	Swimming
Pupils should:	Pupils should:	Pupils should:	Pupils should:	Pupils should:	If swimming is taught in key stage 1, teaching of the early parts of the programmes of study set out in key stage 2 should be considered first.
● experience and be encouraged to take part in running, jumping and throwing activities, concentrating on accuracy, speed, height, length and distance.	● experience and develop control, co-ordination, balance, poise and elevation in basic actions including travelling, jumping, turning, gesture and stillness. ● explore contrasts of speed, tension, continuity, shape, size, direction and level and describe what they have done. ● experience working with a range and variety of contrasting stimuli, including music. ● be given opportunities to explore moods and feelings through spontaneous responses and through structured tasks. ● be helped to develop rhythmic responses. ● experience, and be guided towards, making dances with clear beginnings, middles and ends.	● experience using a variety of games equipment including, where appropriate, specially designed equipment for pupils with physical disabilities. ● experience, practise and develop a variety of ways of sending, receiving and travelling with a ball. ● experience elements of games play that include chasing, dodging, avoiding and awareness of space and other players. ● be given opportunities to make up and play games with simple rules and objectives that involve one person and a limited amount of equipment, extended to working with a partner when ready.	● experience many ways of performing the basic actions of travelling, turning, rolling, jumping, balancing, swinging, climbing and taking weight on hands, both on the floor and using apparatus. ● be given opportunities to practise, adapt and improve their control of individual actions. ● be given opportunities to link together a series of actions both on the floor and using apparatus, and be able to repeat them. ● be taught to carry and position simple apparatus using the correct lifting technique.	● explore the potential for physical activities within the immediate environment. ● undertake simple orientation activities. ● apply physical skills out of doors on suitable equipment. ● develop an awareness of basic safety practices.	

Key stage 1: End of key stage statements and programme of study (general)

End of key stage statements	Programme of study (general)	Examples
By the end of the key stage pupils should be able to:	Pupils should:	Pupils should:
a) plan and perform safely a range of simple actions and linked movements in response to given tasks and stimuli.	1) be given opportunities to develop a wide range of simple movements in a variety of activities with and without equipment.	*jump; roll; run; lift; climb or use adaptations and interpretations of these movements where necessary.*
	2) be encouraged to recognise and make up simple rules, and work within them.	*be taught the Green Cross Code and Water Safety Code; stop with control on a signal; be taught not to enter the pool until told; make up rules for a simple activity with bat and ball.*
	3) be guided and encouraged to use movement to show moods and feelings and respond to simple rhythms and contrasting stimuli.	*respond imaginatively to words or other means of communication including music, poetry and stories as stimuli to contrasting movement qualities.*
	4) be taught to link movements with increasing control to show changes of direction or levels and variations of speed, tension or rhythm.	*jump followed by a roll to finish standing up; travel followed by a turn.*
	5) be helped to recognise and follow safety procedures, including lifting, carrying and moving equipment.	*be encouraged to use equipment with care; decide what to wear for a walk; decide that the apparatus is appropriately positioned.*
b) practise and improve their performance.	1) be encouraged to practise and perform simple skills.	*project objects in a variety of ways with increasing accuracy; roll a ball at a target; dribble a ball with hands or feet; concentrate on distance when jumping.*
	2) be encouraged to improve performance as they work alone and, when ready, in co-operation with a partner.	*concentrate on showing contrasting shapes as they move; throw a ball to a partner who hits it back with a bat.*
c) describe what they and others are doing.	1) be given the opportunity to describe what they and others have done in physical education, and how they did it, using simple, functional and aesthetic terms.	*notice whether the movements are smooth or jerky; identify the difference between leaping and hopping actions; say how well they and others have landed; indicate that a dance was happy or sad.*
d) recognise the effects of physical activity on their bodies.	1) be made aware of the changes that happen to their bodies during exercise.	*detect that their heart is beating faster, breathing is more rapid and that they become hotter during exercise.*

Note: the wording has been taken directly from the National Curriculum document but the numbering has been added by the authors for ease of reference when using the Lesson Plans.

CORE MOVEMENT SKILLS FOR KEY STAGE 1

CORE MOVEMENTS AT KEY STAGE 1

There are a number of core movements that form the basis of the physical education curriculum. These are essential at Key Stage 1 and it is therefore important to clarify the essential aspects of each of these movements. They are broken down into stages which enables the teacher to facilitate and assess learning. You will find them referred to throughout the lesson plans by numbers. It is important that you understand the basic movement skills involved in PE, and time spent studying these core movements will be time well spent.

Activity 1: Walking

Immature phase

In this phase there is an uneven, unco-ordinated stride pattern. The feet may be displaced inwards or outwards. The arms hang at the sides and do not assist the action. Bodily movement is not in an upright position.

Intermediate phase

In this phase the stride pattern is becoming co-ordinated. The feet placement begins to show lift and transference of weight. The arms begin to complement the leg action. The posture of the body is now beginning to show tension and the correct direction of movement.

Mature phase

The weight is transferred from one foot to the other with the toes pointing in the direction of travel. As one foot is placed on the floor the other one is raised slightly and so leaves contact with the floor before a reversal process takes place. The arms are at the sides swinging forward and back in opposition to the movement of the feet. The body is upright showing good posture.

Activity 2: Running

Immature phase

This stage is typified by an uneven unco-ordinated stride which has no flight phase. The leg action tends to be 'out and around' from the hip which enables the child to maintain balance more effectively. The arms tend to be held outward and have a small range of movement.

Intermediate phase

The support leg extends at take-off and thus increases the flight phase. The stride length also increases and the arms swing more vigorously vertically and with less horizontal movement.

Mature phase

The knee is raised high and swings forward quickly. The knee of the support leg bends slightly. There is a great increase in the flight phase and the length of the stride. The arms swing in opposition to the legs.

Activity 3: Stopping

Immature phase

There is difficulty in controlling the body. The child is unable to stop immediately at the appropriate point in a practice or game. There is a lack of reaction to visual or sound stimuli and minimal body tension. The movement of the arms and legs is inappropriate. The body is not at rest.

Intermediate phase

The child is able to respond to instruction but difficulties in maintaining whole body stillness are shown in slight upper body and head movement.

Mature phase

The two feet are placed firmly on the floor with the weight evenly distributed. Tension promotes stillness throughout the body with the head focusing on the direction of travel, creating an upright posture.

Activity 4: Jumping

Immature phase

The arms are not co-ordinated with the jump, they are simply used to maintain balance. The trunk is mainly projected upwards for height, but not forward for distance. At take-off and landing the child has difficulty in using both feet simultaneously.

Intermediate phase

The arms initiate the jump with upward movement. The trunk is again mainly vertical in movement. There is a greater extension from the hips, knees and ankles at take-off; these remain quite bent during flight.

Mature phase

The arms move backwards and then forwards just prior to take-off. The arms are held high throughout the jump. The trunk is propelled at 45°, giving major emphasis to the horizontal direction of the jump. The hips, legs and ankles are completely extended at take-off.

Activity 5: Hopping

Immature Phase

The leg hardly leaves the floor. There is a complete lack of co-ordination with upper and lower body. The non-hopping foot can remain constantly in contact with the floor. The upper part of the body tends to lean forward. There is a complete lack of appropriate arm action to aid elevation and balance.

Intermediate phase

There is a hopping action but it is not easily maintained, due to lack of awareness of upper body and lower body movement. There is limited use of the arms to assist elevation and balance.

Mature phase
One foot is continually lifted from the floor. The knees are slightly bent to assist elevation of the body and to support landing. There is tension of the body, particularly the hopping leg. The posture is upright, with back straight. The head is facing forwards and the arms are by the sides with elbows bent to assist elevation and the balance of the hop. The non-hopping leg should be bent at the knee and held at that position during the hop to either assist hop or help elevation.

Activity 6: Skipping
This movement needs to be introduced after the progression of the hopping action.

Immature phase
There is a lack of co-ordination of the alternate leg and arm action. The body posture lacks tension and position to assist flight. The knees and toes are not straight or stretched.

Intermediate phase
There is an improvement in co-ordination but a lack of knee lift and poor leg position. There is limited spring in the elevation. The arms are by the sides and bent but have little movement to assist elevation. The movement becomes progressively more fluid.

Mature phase
The arms should be held away from the sides of the body and should be slightly bent with a forward, backward swing to help the momentum of the body. The body tension is similar to the hop. The leg action is an alternate movement from one foot to the other in which the whole body is stretched in the spring. The knees are straight and the toes are pointed towards the floor. It should be a fluent and rhythmic action.

DANCE

ABOUT DANCE

Dance is part of the cultural heritage of all people, whether this be as a social experience (for example, the disco) or as a theatrical experience (for example, a visit to see a professional company). The kind of dance that is performed varies with time and place (for example, the dances of Tudor England are not those of today and the dances performed in Ghana are not the same as those of Bali). Wherever dance occurs, and in whatever form, the following strands of involvement can be found: the performer/dancer, the maker/composer and the observer/audience; in Western cultures the spectator role often predominates but if all those who go to discos are included there is also a very large performer role. Today British society consists of people from very varied cultural (including dance) traditions, and each of these has a part to play in the development of dance in the 1990s; at times styles retain their distinctiveness (for example, Lancashire morris) and at others new styles emerge as aspects of several different dances are brought together.

Whatever the characteristics of any dance there is always movement organised in time and space. Creators of dance shape and structure these elements in the ways most appropriate for their purpose (for example, to enliven a festive occasion, to communicate some universal truth or to fulfil a religious function). Movements are selected because they make pleasing lines or rhythms or for their contribution to the idea being expressed.

Dance in schools should introduce pupils to, and develop understanding of, this diversity. This can be done by providing opportunities for pupils to dance, to make dances and to watch the dance of others including professional works. In these ways pupils can be led to express their own ideas through dance, to share these ideas with others and to see their own endeavours in the wider context of the adult world.

Children at Key Stage 1 respond spontaneously to rhythmic beats; they jump for joy and stamp their feet in anger; already they possess the tools necessary for success in dance. Within formal education they need to be helped to structure these natural responses into the art form of dance and this can be done through introducing them to the three strands of dance education: composing, performing and evaluating, or quite simply: making, doing and describing what they and others have done.

Progression

In dance there is not a simple line of development where one skill is a prerequisite for another. Indeed, in each of the units of work and within an individual lesson, children will be having several different experiences; for example, in lesson 1 of this area of activity they are:

- responding to music
- acquiring skill in controlling the action
- being helped to develop rhythmic responses by keeping in time
- learning to repeat and to practise.

It is also the case that some experiences will be repeated later in the unit but that there will be greater expectations in terms of pupil response. For example, there is an emphasis on body shape in most lessons of unit 1 as this helps to clarify the dance action, but by lesson 7 pupils are expected to be able to choose and link shapes, whereas in lesson 1 they copy the teacher.

Progression can take several forms; for example, throughout Key Stage 1 it should be possible to see the following:

1 Increasing ability to make the movement clear in shape and rhythm.
2 Tasks become more difficult; e.g. in unit 1, lesson 1, pupils march anywhere; in unit 2, lesson 1 they have to travel on a pathway they can repeat.
3 Children becoming less dependent on the teacher; e.g. in early lessons they copy the teacher; later they are required to make shapes for themselves.
4 The children's ability to concentrate on the task should increase.
5 Ability to control the body parts and rhythm should increase.
6 Children should be better able to remember from one week to another.

NATIONAL CURRICULUM REQUIREMENTS AT KEY STAGE 1

The following end of key stage statements are most applicable to dance:

> Pupils should be able to:
>
> a) plan and perform safely a range of simple actions and linked movements in response to given tasks and stimuli.
> b) practise and improve their performance.
> c) describe what they and others are doing.

The programme of study (general) indicates how the teacher might assist pupils to develop these skills and understanding in dance as follows:

> Pupils should:
>
> a1) be given opportunities to develop a wide range of simple movements in a variety of activities with and without equipment.
> a3) be guided and encouraged to use movement to show moods and feelings and respond to simple rhythms and contrasting stimuli.
> a4) be taught to link movements with increasing control to show changes of direction or levels and variations of speed, tension or rhythm.
> b1) be encouraged to practise and perform simple skills.
> b2) be encouraged to improve performance as they work alone and, when ready, in co-operation with a partner.
> c1) be given the opportunity to describe what they and others have done in physical education, and how they did it, using simple, functional and aesthetic terms.

The programme of study (activity specific) identifies the content of these experiences as follows:

> Pupils should:
>
> •   experience and develop control, co-ordination, balance, poise and elevation in basic actions including travelling, jumping, turning, gesture and stillness.
> •   explore contrasts of speed, tension, continuity, shape, size, direction and level and describe what they have done.
> •   experience working with a range and variety of contrasting stimuli, including music.
> •   be given opportunities to explore moods and feelings through spontaneous responses and through structured tasks.
> •   be helped to develop rhythmic responses.
> •   experience, and be guided towards, making dances with clear beginnings, middles and ends.

TEACHING DANCE AT KEY STAGE 1

The emphasis at this key stage is on the provision of opportunities for pupils to have a variety of experiences and to practise what they are doing. In these ways children are gaining the dance vocabulary which forms the basis of future development, and are acquiring good working habits (e.g. making connections between the movements they are doing and the stimulus which motivated them to make the movements). As with all other aspects of the physical education curriculum it is important that, even at this early stage, the children are involved in the three processes of making decisions about what they are going to do, carrying out the actions and thinking about how successful they have been. In the model lessons there is an indication of which of these three processes is in focus at a particular

point. This has not been demonstrated for every lesson in the units because the conciseness of the statements often embodies all three process; for example: 'Make a funny shape for teddy' requires a judgement about what makes something funny, decision-making about what the body should do to achieve this and then carrying through the plan in performance.

The lesson plans
It would be inappropriate to isolate the requirements of the programme of study into discrete units. Any dance lesson requires a stimulus for movement and attention to the action, dynamic and spatial content; therefore each lesson contains work in which all of these come together. Two principles underly the selection of

content: firstly the need to develop understanding of the material out of which dances can be formed and secondly the need to make dances. Both are equally important and in practice this is merely a question of emphasis, at times on content itself, at others on its use to fulfil a particular purpose.

Therefore most lessons have two themes: the stimulus (expressive content) and the vocabulary (dance content). Whilst this is a totally artificial division it is felt to be helpful to the teacher. The stimuli for the lessons are representative of a range of different starting points from which dances can be made. They include: pictures, poetry, prose, events and objects. In addition, they take account of the need both to make links with the National Curriculum for art and for music and to include dances which arise from material relevant to the wide variety of cultural traditions present in today's society. Where music has been suggested from a particular source it is because these tapes provide, in addition to the given piece, many others useful for the dance teacher. The ideas presented are neither exhaustive nor definitive; many other starting points could equally well have been chosen. The important factor is whether the starting point is motivating for the pupils and also has potential for dance; i.e. action is an integral part of the idea.

In following the lessons these points should be kept in mind:

1 Pupils and teacher need the security of a clear movement framework.

2 In the early stages of learning the action should always be accompanied by some audible rhythm, e.g. in unit 1 lesson 2:

1	2	3	4	1	2	3	4
jump	h	o	l	d	jump	jump	sink to floor

3 Pupils need to have their attention drawn to what the movement is saying as well as to how it is being performed. This can be done in several ways, for example: by using words such as 'creep' instead of 'walk', by giving illustrations such as '*like* a bouncing ball' or 'light as a feather' and by providing concrete images such as Mighty Muscle in unit 1, lesson 4.

4 Sections should be repeated several (perhaps four) times without a pause, then pupils can be given advice followed by further repetition.

5 There is a need for balance between increasing the range of vocabulary pupils have to use and increasing their skill in using it.

All of the above have been assumed in writing the lesson plans, although in the model lessons they are made explicit.

The amount of material included for each lesson is based upon the mythical average Key Stage 1 pupil, but any particular class of pupils may take a shorter or longer time to cover the same content. In all cases the sequencing does assume knowledge of material included in former lessons, but where one lesson in absolutely dependent on the previous one this is indicated by 'continued' after the theme.

The units are supported by two activity banks, the Core Movement Skills Bank and the Dance Activity Bank. These provide further details of the stimulus and accompaniment and secondly, they provide additional information to assist the development of pupil learning either in respect of particular skills or in making the connection between movement and meaning.

Professional work as a resource

An important aspect of dance teaching is the need to relate the pupils' experiences to the wider world of dance. This is often not easy to do as videos are not always obtainable and it is difficult to take a class of this age to a live performance. However, the impetus that such events give to the children's work is tremendous and whenever it does become possible the opportunity should be taken. The units do include several instances where this would be particularly appropriate and these are clearly noted within the resources for the lesson.

The model lessons

The two lessons have been chosen because they exemplify two rather different approaches to dance teaching, i.e. that contained in the lesson 'bag of bones' where the main focus of the lesson is on developing dance vocabulary (awareness of the ways in which parts of the body can move) and that in 'Starry Night' where the main focus is on developing appropriate responses to the painting.

Within each lesson a few features have been identified because they exemplify aspects of good dance teaching; they are neither definitive nor exhaustive, but should be considerations when planning all dance lessons, even though as in these two lessons emphases are different.

Model lesson 1

Use of accompaniment is an important feature of dance work. In the lesson, each time the pupils are asked to move, the teacher provides accompaniment on the tambourine; this should reflect the quality of the action that the children are trying to achieve. In providing this accompaniment the teacher is both giving a very clear structure to the movement, i.e. beginning, middle and end, and also is employing a very good control mechanism, i.e. there is no doubt when pupils should be moving and being still. Appropriate patterns of behaviour are established within the dance convention of phrasing rather than having to be imposed from the outside.

It is important to ensure that the children are given clear action tasks, e.g. shake the body, and therefore all have a very definite goal to achieve. The tasks are capable of achievement at many different levels of ability so all pupils are given the opportunity of success.

Once the pupils have begun to give some action response to the task they need help with how to improve. This can be done in two ways: firstly by extending the number of things they can do and secondly by improving the way in which they do the movements they choose. In relation to the former, for example, first they copy the teacher doing lots of different actions, e.g. shrugging shoulders, wriggling fingers, the teacher then suggests they use different body parts, and finally they have to make one part very important; the onus is gradually moving from the teacher to the pupil. In relation to the latter, the children have their attention drawn to particular aspects, e.g. making the action bouncy or making a clear end; they are given definite things on which to concentrate.

Decision making and planning are important skills. It is important to provide the children both with the tools which will enable them to make decisions and the opportunity to use these tools to serve their own purposes. Therefore in this lesson they work with the teacher whilst exploring lots of different ways of using the body before having to choose their own way. They will have been given lots of ideas before as a class they have to decide how to end the dance.

Evaluation of performance needs to be built in from the start of dance work. Even at this early stage of the children's experience they should be thinking about what they have been doing and checking that it fulfils the requirements of the task, i.e. they should be making a judgement, however simple. For example in this lesson they are asked 'Can I see the difference between the escape and the bounce?' and 'Can I see which part is moving?'. In both these cases the pupils have to think about what they have been doing and make a judgement against criteria which have been made clear earlier in the lesson.

Do not forget the importance of the conclusion. The conclusion of this lesson provides both a body 'cool down' after an energetic lesson and also gives the children an opportunity to become calm before going to the next lesson; both of these considerations are important in every lesson.

Model lesson 1: Reception/Year 1, unit 1, lesson 3 ▷

Theme: bag of bones; body co-ordination

Purpose: PoS General a1, a4, b2

Activity bank: Core: 2, 3

Resources: music: *Popcorn* by Gershon/Kingsley; tambourine; model skeleton if available

Activity	Organisation	Teaching points
Introduction: Travel by bouncing around the room.	Start in their own space.　(!) Give steady rhythm on tambourine, 16 beats.	Show me your starting position.　(PL) Look for a space; bounce lightly as if ball; keep on toes, bend knees.　(P)
On change, shake whole body and hold in.	Shake tambourine for equivalent of 8 beats.	Make whole body shake: hands, arms legs, middle. Hold action quite still at the end; hold breath.　(P)
	Repeat at least four times continuously.	
Repeat the above bouncing in towards teacher, shaking when close to teacher, then going away again.	Repeat rhythm above. When children come in towards you make sure they are not too close.　(!) Practise clapping in time to the music.　(P)	Listen carefully to the rhythm; try to make the whole action light and fun-like; let the whole body join in the bouncing.　(P)
Repeat with music.	Accompany with tambourine as above.	Listen to the music. Keep to the beat. Show your starting position. Be still when you finish.　(P)
Development: In own space in time to music copy teacher nodding head, shrugging shoulders, bending/stretching knees and elbows. Wriggle hips, shake whole body.	Put on music. Children copy teacher. Make sure they are all facing.	Keep every movement light, bouncy.　(P) Keep in time with the beat. Try to make one part of the body very important.　(PL)
Choose two of the above and change from one to another (phrase A).　(PL)	Use tambourine and change the sound to indicate change of body part.	Make the part very clear.　(PL) Listen for the change in the sound of the tambourine.

Use pupil demonstration.		Who can tell me which body parts were being used? (EV)
Start with the whole body tucked in; stretch out one limb and bring it back in again. Repeat with other limbs (phrase B).	Give slow sound on tambourine, then sharp sound for drawing in. Repeat at least four times continuously.	Imagine the limb is trying to escape from the bag; it is sneaking out, trying not to be seen; only one part moves at a time. (PL)
Start with phrase B and add phrase A, then bouncing all around the room.	Put on music but use tambourine to help children know when to change idea.	Imagine the bones get out of the bag and are excited. (PL) Make the body parts very clear. Listen to the music. (P)
Practise lots of times.	Put on music. Talk to pupils through the changes. Use tambourine to signal.	Make each movement very clear. Keep everything light and energetic. (P)
Discuss with pupils how the dance should end, e.g. the bones are caught and get put back in the bag or go wild and fall down exhausted. (PL)		
Practise the end.		Be still until the music is switched off. (P) Can I see the different parts of the story in your movements? (EV)
Perform several times.	Each time give some point to think about.	E.g. can I see which body part is moving? Is the escape different from the bounce? (EV)

Conclusion:

Reach up high, curl up small with one body part very important.	Do the actions with the pupils.	Breathe out as curl up. Be very gentle. (P)
Tell teacher which body parts have been used.	Encourage pupils to talk about what they have done. (EV)	

Model lesson 2

The distinguishing feature of a dance lesson is the use of movement either to 'say' something, or as a response to a particular stimulus. The main focus of this lesson is to help the children look closely at the chosen picture and to show the results of their observations through their movement response. The teacher helps the children by drawing their attention to some particular aspects of the painting, e.g. the smoke rising, by providing them with the opportunity to answer structured questions and then giving them a clear movement framework within which to try out their movements, e.g. 'rise up until stretched high into the air and whizz down to the ground again'. On several occasions in the lesson they are asked what it feels like to move in different ways, or how they would feel in certain circumstances. These kinds of questions help the pupils to make connections between the actual movement they are making and the effect they are hoping to create whilst performing the actions.

Children need always to be encouraged to improve their performance, firstly by phrasing the movement. At this stage of experience when pupils are trying to make their movements 'like' something else they need help in organising their responses so that they perform actions which have some definition. To do this the teacher needs to provide the structure, for example 'rise up until stretched high into the air and whizz down to the ground'. This example shows how the children's movement is clarified in terms of time, level and action because of the words used by the teacher but there is still plenty of opportunity for each child to do the phrase in their own way.

The second way of improving the children's performance is by helping them to extend their response. After the pupils have begun to move the teacher needs to make suggestions about how these movements could be improved, for example, 'Make your floor pattern clear'. Suggestions like this can be reinforced by getting the children to practise just the one part and helping them to do it better. These suggestions can be used by all the pupils whatever they are doing but each interprets the suggestion in their own way.

In lessons where pupils are helped to observe something and then take the ideas into their own movement, decision making is a very important aspect of the lesson. Note the use of leading questions when referring to last week's lesson, the use of questions which require the pupils to check that their actions are a response to the painting, and the use of very clear proposals for making changes. Children have to make choices all the way through the lesson. Firstly they have to choose what to do and secondly out of all the possible ideas they have tried they have to choose a few that best fulfil the task.

Evaluating is again an important feature of the lesson. In one sense the whole lesson is about making judgements as to whether or not the movements that are being made are a real response to the painting. They are asked to observe what is in the picture and assess whether their movements are like this feature, e.g. the smoke. They are asked to check their own movements for whether they meet expectations, e.g. 'Is the 'whizz' different from the 'drift'?' requires that even when they know what the words mean they have to be able to decide if their movements do look different from each other, i.e. a judgement. At the end of the lesson half the class watch the other half and are asked to identify pupils who are performing particularly well in respect of particular parts of the task, e.g. 'look for pupils who really make their movements look as if they were frightened'. Such a question requires pupils to make two kinds of judgement: firstly what kind of movement suggests 'fright' and secondly which pupils are best doing this. Note that pupils' observation and judgements are closely channelled by the nature of the questions asked.

After a period of viewing such as this there is no need for a further 'cool down'.

Do not forget the importance of cross-curricular links in dance. There are two obvious links in this lesson, with Art and English.

The starting point for the lesson is a painting by Van Gogh and this provides an opportunity for the children to look closely at some particular aspects of the painting, e.g. the use of darker and lighter sections. The need to make movements which match certain features of the painting requires close observation of what is actually there and thus provides good training for looking at other works. It would be possible to extend this lesson further by learning something about Van Gogh as a person or by looking at some of his other paintings and perhaps asking the children to make their own paintings based on what they have observed.

The English attainment target of speaking and listening also figures predominantly. The children are required to talk about what they see in the painting and how their movements fit in with aspects of the painting. They can also be required to listen carefully to what the teacher and other pupils say. Throughout the lesson they have to respond to simple instructions given by the teacher. In addition there are abundant opportunities for increasing vocabulary both in order that the pupils understand the task set and by encouraging them to use a wide range of words in their replies to questions.

Model lesson 2: Year 2, unit 1, lesson 4

Theme: Van Gogh's painting *Starry Night* (continued); combining pattern and mood

Purpose: PoS General a3, a4, b2, c1

Resources: colour print of *Starry Night* by Vincent Van Gogh; music: *Neptune* from *The Planets Suite* by Gustav Holst; tambourine

Activity	Organisation	Teaching points
Introduction: Show picture and ask questions about what was done in lesson 3.	Pupils sitting on floor near teacher and where they can see picture.	What shapes did we make? Show me where these are in the picture. How did we make the dark parts different from the light parts? What did you tell me it felt like when you were out in the dark? (EV)
Get into a space on your own and show me some of the movements you did last week.	Ensure pupils are well spaced out. Accompany with short phrase on tambourine, e.g. a shaking sound with a single beat to signal the stop. Change the sound sometimes: louder/softer/quicker/slower.	Have a clear starting position. Listen to the sound. Have some stronger and some more gentle parts; make your floor pattern clear. When the sound stops make sure you are very still. Is your body making a shape that is in the picture? (PL)
Repeat lots of times.	Give one teaching point on each repeat.	

13

Repeat some of the actions you have just done but this time show me how you would do them if you were frightened. (PL)

Change the sound of the accompaniment to match the mood, but continue to mark the end of the phrase with a single beat.

Make your starting position; show me you are frightened. (PL)
Look where you are going; tread carefully on the floor; travel very quickly as if running away; freeze as you come to stillness. Change direction as if trying not to be followed. Spread the body, skip/gallop, keep high in the air, look outwards, add turns/jumps (phrase A). (P)

Repeat, showing how you would do this if enjoying being in the dark. (PL)

Development:

Look at the smoke shape; ask pupils to tell you what it looks like.

Bring children in close so they can see the picture.

Encourage use of extensive vocabulary.

Move into a space of your own. Tuck up close to the floor; rise up until stretched high into the air; whizz down to the ground again.

Accompany with tambourine: eight taps for the rise and a long shake for the whizz down. Repeat at least four times continuously.

Be very gentle as you use the part of the body leading the action. (P)
Try other parts of the body; try to make the movement like smoke rising on a very still day. (PL)
Whizz down to the ground as fast as you can. What are your arms doing? Which part of the body do you tuck up on when you reach the floor? (EV)

Repeat with music.

Use tambourine over the music to help pupils keep the phrasing.

Repeat the above, but shoot upwards and drift downwards.

Accompany with tambourine: a short sharp shake for the shoot up and a long series of taps for the drift down.

Can you get to the top by the time the sound stops? Take a long time to come down as slowly as you can. Add a turn. (PL)
What shape is the body making? Which part of the body do you tuck up on? (EV)

Repeat at least four times continuously.

Repeat with music.

Use tambourine over the music to help pupils keep phrasing.

Ask pupils what it feels like when they are rising, whizzing, shooting and drifting. (EV)

Pupils sit on floor.

Encourage pupils to use 'real' and invented words and images to capture the feeling of the movement. (X)

Pupils choose their favourite combination of upward and downward movements and perform with music. (PL)

Put on music.

Make your movements really show me some of the things we talked about. (PL)

Pupils choose either the 'frightened' or the 'enjoying' movements (phrase A) practised in the introduction. (PL)
Perform with music.

Put on music.

Make sure I can see changes in the movements you have chosen: have you been near the floor/high in the air? Have you had turns/leaps? (PL)

Half class perform 'smoke' phrase while other half surround them with phrase A.

Divide class in half.
One half comes close together in the middle of the room; the others spread out round them.

Remember which part you are doing and keep doing this; don't copy anyone else. (P)

Hold clear starting position, then perform own movements lots of times with the music.

Put on music, and also accompany with tambourine to assist phrasing.

Can I see which movements you chose? Can I tell from your movements what they felt like? (EV)

Change over and repeat.

Conclusion:

Half class (i.e. half of each group) perform the dance; the other half watch.	Pupils watching come to the front of the class, sit on floor and tuck feet in.	Look for pupils who have the clearest shapes/pathways. Look for pupils who shoot/whizz really well; can you tell me what it is about their movements that shows this? Look for pupils who really make their movements look as if they were frightened; can you tell me what it is about their movements that shows this? (EV)

DANCE ACTIVITY BANK

Activity 1: Safety

Spacing

It is always necessary to ensure that the pupils have enough space around them in which to move without contacting other pupils, unless this is the purpose of the lesson. They should from the very first lesson look around themselves and check that they are not too near other pupils. This is especially important when travelling from one place to another. Speed should be contained within limits compatible with safety. When the dance requires that children 'dash' away, this section should first be practised at slow speed with awareness of the spacing and then put into the dance context. Particular care needs to be taken when the pupils are being encouraged to travel backwards. They should look in the direction in which they are travelling.

Landing and falling to the ground

Falling is an exciting dance image for children, as for example in unit 2, lesson 5 (page 28), where the dance requires that Freddy Frog falls off his lily pad. It is however also an action which requires great attention to the safety aspects, particularly at this age, otherwise pupils could very easily bang their heads. It is suggested that the pupils practise this skill in the following stages:

- ensure pupils can land safely on their feet
- land and then sit down carefully on the floor; as skill increases gradually decrease the gap between landing and sitting
- from sitting, roll backwards and shake feet in the air (be sure to check children are rounding their backs); return to sitting
- join the above together with a pause between each section and gradually decrease the length of the gap
- as pupils become proficient increase the speed.

General warning

There are many actions which are performed in the dance context which would be very unsafe if performed outside the controlled conditions of the lesson, e.g. leaping on lily pads. It is important that on every such occasion pupils are reminded that they are on no account to practise the actions elsewhere.

Activity 2: Working for poise

From the very earliest stages pupils should be encouraged to work for good quality dance action. The following points may help in achieving this; they should be an expectation, if not an achievement from the very first lesson.

In all the pupils' movement look for the things shown in the picture above, i.e. the way the action goes all the way to the toes, the middle of the body is held firm, the head is looking at the hands and there is a lot of concentration.

15

The picture at the foot of the previous page illustrates some more points that may help to improve the pupils' action. Look for the aliveness of the action right through to the fingertips, the way the head is in line with the body and the eyes are looking outwards, the way the tummy is held well braced, and the way the back leg is fully involved in the action. There is full concentration on the movement.

Activity 3: The phrase
This is a sequence of movement with a clear beginning, middle and end. In the early stages of developing an idea it is important that the action is accompanied by audible rhythm such as percussion or music.

Example 1, from unit 1, lesson 5 (page 23)
Use the voice to indicate the rhythm given below:

float up and up and up, and toss, and toss, and toss, and s e t t l e   a n d   burst.

Example 2, from unit 1, lesson 8 (page 25)
The actions occur on each word of the chorus of the carol as shown below.

We	will	rock	you,	rock	you	rock	you
step	step	step	step	step	step	and	stop

We	will	rock	you,	rock	you	rock	you
step	step	step	step	step	step	and	stop

We	will	bring	a	coat	of	fur
Lift	present	high	into	the	air	

Darling	darling	little	lamb
Gently	place	it	on	the	ground

Activity 4: Mighty muscle
To give an impression of strength pupils need to:

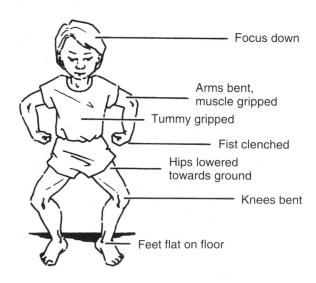

- Focus down
- Arms bent, muscle gripped
- Tummy gripped
- Fist clenched
- Hips lowered towards ground
- Knees bent
- Feet flat on floor

The following practices might help:

- lean against a wall and try to push it away; use different body parts for the pushing
- lie on the floor and push body away from it; try the whole body, or parts of the body in turn
- push against a partner

Here are some other things strong people do:

In each case pupils' attention should be drawn to the following:

- how the feet are placed on the floor
- the line of the body
- whether the knees are bent or straight
- where the hips are placed
- where the energy is coming from and going to
- where the hands are placed.

Pupils should then be asked to try to reproduce these in their own movement.

Activity 5: Bubbles
To achieve an impression of lightness pupils need to: look up, extend the limbs away from the body, let the chest lead upwards, breathe in gently, stretch the legs, be on their toes and have their feet close together.

The following practices might help:

- stand on tip-toe and look up
- breathe in gently and feel the chest rise
- feel air underneath the arm-pits and let the hands rise upwards
- grip the muscles in a position near the floor, gradually release the tension and rise upwards.

Activity 6: Transforming a character into dance

Whenever pupils are required to make a dance phrase around any character, animal or imaginary person the following questions will help them to transform the real thing into the actions and qualities of the dance.

What do they look like and how do they move?

Using the example of Thunderbirds and Tracy Island, ask the pupils to show you in their movement the answers to the following questions. How do they stand? How are the feet placed on the floor? How are the shoulders set? How are the limbs jointed? How do they walk? How do the legs move? How do the arms move? How does the head move?

What do they do?

Using the example of Thunderbirds and Tracy Island, answers might include the following; they help other people, they man International Rescue, they ride in rockets and submarines, they use chutes to enter things, they use revolving doors, they have magic powers, they do dangerous things.

Pupils then make short dance phrases which try to show the things that are done through their movement.

Activity 7: Pathways

Pupils could choose one of these or many others.

They could draw their own or do rubbings or objects and dance the patterns. They could join several together, or they could draw the route from the school gate to the classroom. For example

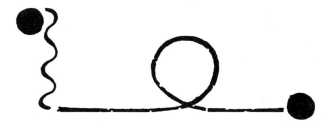

Activity 8: Chinese New Year

The Hearth God, Tsao-Wang, watches over the house all year noting who is bad and who is good. Just before the Chinese New Year (sometime between 20th January and 20th February) he goes to give a report in heaven and this determines whether or not the family will have good luck for the following year. He returns on the first day of the New Year and special fire crackers are let off to make sure he gets back to the house. During his absence the house has been cleaned from top to bottom and red paper strips are hung on either side of the door. Everyone celebrates his return with processions and dances including the Dragon and Lion Dances.

17

If there is a nearby Chinese community it might be possible for some-one to come in and tell the pupils stories about the Chinese New Year ceremonies. Pupils could visit a traditional ceremony and see the Dragon Dance being performed; they could then compare their own dance with the real version. Pupils could make masks, banners and the dragon costume.

Further ideas can be obtained in *Chinese New Year* published by the Multicultural Education and Language Service, Broadbent Road, Oldham OL1 4JU in 1988.

Activity 9: Draw a score

This could be done before or after making the dance. For example, for the balloon dance, unit 2, lesson 7 (page 29), this might be a suitable score:

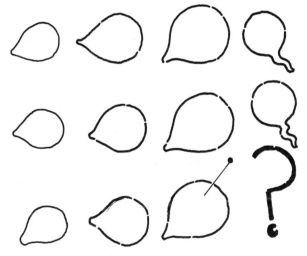

This activity relates directly to the National Curriculum for Music Attainment Target 1 Performing and Composing 'xi) use and understand simple signs and symbols for musical sounds when composing'.

Activity 10: *The Magic Drum*

The full story can be found in *African Myths and Legends* by K. Arnott published by Oxford University Press, 1989. The aspects of the story which are used in the dance are summarised below.

Once upon a time there was a very rich king. He had a very big family and everyone in his kingdom was happy and contented. The main cause of the king's wealth was a magic drum. Whenever the king beat on his drum large quantities of delicious food appeared on the table. There was so much that he was able to feed his entire kingdom including all the wild animals. Everyone wanted a drum like that of the king so he kept it very well guarded.

There was however a secret about the drum that only the king knew. This was that it would only provide food if its owner had not walked over a stick lying on the path or if he had never crossed a fallen tree trunk. If the owner had done either of these things three hundred warriors would come and beat the guests at the table until they cried for mercy.

One day the king was tricked into giving his drum away, but he was not too worried because he knew that sooner or later the new owner would walk over a stick. Sure enough that did happen and the drum was swiftly returned to the king and his people lived happily ever after.

Traditionally dances of this kind would be accompanied by live drumming; in the early stages the teacher playing the drum would be most appropriate. Changes in the dance are signalled by a particular sound from the drummer; drummer and dancers are very closely linked in many African cultures. Two possible sources of pre-recorded accompaniment are given on p. 30. Alternatively it might be possible to get the services of a drummer from the one of the local communities.

Activity 11: *Seven Springs*

Seven Springs is a traditional folk dance. It should be noted that this is just one of the many ways that this dance can be performed.

The pupils walk round in a circle clockwise for fifteen steps and then stop; two steps to each bar, stopping in the last bar. Then they jump off both feet and then stamp the right foot heavily. The walking round is repeated each time adding one more action as follows:

second time	stamp right foot, then stamp left foot
third time	stamp right foot, then stamp left foot, then kneel on right knee
fourth time	stamp right foot, then stamp left foot, then kneel on right knee, then kneel on left knee
fifth time	stamp right foot, then stamp left foot, then kneel on right knee, then kneel on left knee, then place right elbow on the ground
sixth time	stamp right foot, then stamp left foot, then kneel on right knee, then kneel on left knee, then place right elbow on the ground, then place left elbow on the ground
seventh time	stamp right foot, then stamp left foot, then kneel on right knee, then kneel on left knee, then place right elbow on the ground, then place left elbow on the ground, then lie flat on the ground.

Here is the music.

SEVEN SPRINGS

Activity 12: *Trainers*

The poem *Trainers* by Michael Rosen appears in *DON'T Put Mustard in the Custard* first published by Andre Deutsch Children's Books, an imprint of Scholastic Publications Ltd.

Trainers

See me in my trainers
speeding round the house
see me in my trainers
speeding down the street
see me in my trainers
speeding to the shops

Ask the pupils to look at the line of the body, the angle of the legs, how the arms are used and how they can make it really clear they are 'speeding' without having to go too fast for inside?

see me in my trainers
kicking a tennis ball
see me in my trainers
kicking a hard brick wall

Ask the pupils what it feels like when they have done this. What action in the body do they do? For example, curl up round their tummy, hop on the other foot, shake the foot that hurts.

see me in my trainers
kicking my friend's leg
see me in my trainers
there's a hole in my toe

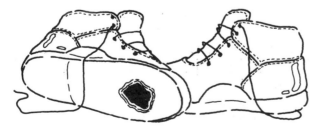

Ask the pupils what position they need to be in to see if there is a hole in their trainers. Are there any other positions they could use to do this? How do they walk when there is a hole in their trainers? What action might they use instead of walking?

see me in my trainers
the sole's worn through
you can't see me in my trainers
they're in the dustbin
See my trainers

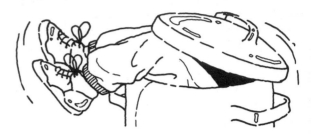

Ask the pupils how they could get this effect in the dance without having a dustbin. Practise balancing with the feet high in the air.

Activity 13: Windy day

The poem *Stocking and Shirt* by James Reeves appears in *That Way and This Poetry for Creative Dance* chosen by F. Baldwin and M. Whitehead and published by Chatto and Windus, London, 1972.

Stocking and Shirt

Can trip and prance,
Though nobody's in them
To make them dance.
See how they waltz
Or minuet,
Watch the petticoat
Pirouette.
This is the dance
Of stocking and shirt,
When the wind puts on
The white lace skirt.
Old clothes and young clothes
Dance together,
Twirling and whirling
In the mad March weather.
'Come!' cries the wind,
To the stocking and shirt,
'Away!' cries the wind
To blouse and skirt.

Then clothes and wind
All pull together,
Across the garden
They suddenly fly
And over the far hedge
High, high, high!

'Stop!' cries the housewife,
But all too late,
Her clothes have passed
The furthest gate.
They are gone for ever
In the bright blue sky,
And only the handkerchiefs
Wave good-bye.

Activity 14: Spring festival

Holi is a Hindu spring festival which is celebrated on the full moon day of the month of Phalgun (February–March). It is the most colourful of the Hindu festivals. There are processions and celebrations, and frequently in the evening preceding the festival bonfires are lit. In some Indian villages mothers carry their children in a circle around a blazing bonfire in the belief that it will help protect the children from danger in the coming year.

An ancient Hindu legend tells the story of the struggle between Prahala and the demon Holika. Prahala was the son of a demon but he chose to worship the god Vishnu. One day Prahala was taken prisoner by Holika and held in a huge bonfire, but before he could be harmed he was rescued by Vishnu and Holika was burnt to death instead.

If there is a near-by South-East Asian community it might be possible for some-one to come in and show the pupils a traditional dance and to explain to them what Holi means to them.

Kathakali hand gestures for use in the dance are:

Get the pupils to sit comfortably on the floor and look at the position of the hands in the diagrams and then try to make their own hands into the same shape. They should try each one in turn and then change to another support, for example kneeling on one knee, and repeat the exercise. Their attention should be drawn to the need to make the position as exact as possible. When they can do this they could repeat the exercise when standing. As they become more proficient they should try to change from one hand position to another. All the time the eyes should look at the hands. As they become more confident they should be encouraged to think about what the rest of the body is doing, could it make a shape that complements that of the hands? Could it surround the hands?

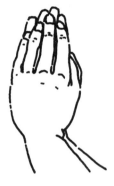

Bud

Opening

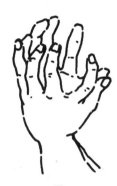

Flower

Flower wilting

LESSON PLANS FOR RECEPTION/YEAR 1 ▶

Unit 1, lesson 1 ▷

Theme: travel and stillness; shape

Purpose: PoS General a1; b1

Activity bank: Core: 1, 3; Dance: 1

Resources: music: *Colonel Hathi's March* (by Sherman) from the film *The Jungle Book*; drum

Introduction:
Copy teacher's shape, e.g. wide, tall.
March around room on drum beat; pupils stop and make a very clear shape.
Repeat: find space of own.
Repeat: make different shape.

Development:
March on the spot: knees high/straight legs/swing arms/soldier-like.
Repeat: skipping instead of marching.
Repeat: travelling around the room; make clear shape on stop.

Teach/practise skipping.
March on the spot, then skip when travelling.
Pupils choose knees high/legs straight; show difference between march and skip.
Practise shapes: wide, long, round. Repeat with clear stillness.

Conclusion:
Yawn into a wide shape; stretch up into a long shape and gradually curl into a little ball.

Unit 1, lesson 2

Theme: jack-in-the-box; contrast in level/elevation

Purpose: PoS General a1, b1

Resources: drum/tambourine/cymbals; toy jack-in-the-box if available

Introduction:
In own space stretch up onto tiptoes; walk gently in and out; stop when drum stops.

Repeat stamping, bending legs.
Change from one to the other, stressing high in the air, low near the ground.

Development:
Lie on floor; tuck up as if hiding.
Jump to feet as if surprised and hold shape in the air.
Repeat slowly coming out to high shape, quickly tucking up.
Repeat varying shape of the body in stillness.

Repeat varying the body part on which weight is taken.
Roll over/crawl/slide before shooting into the air.
Practise jumping into the air and landing on the feet before tucking up; get feeling of excitement.
Start low, jump up into the air, down onto floor, as if hiding; repeat lots of times.

Conclusion:
Stretch into the air and hold; gradually let all the air out of the body and sink to the floor.

Unit 1, lesson 3

Theme: bag of bones; body co-ordination

Purpose: PoS General a1, a4; b2

Activity bank: Core: 2, 3

Resources: music: *Popcorn* by Gershon/Kingsley; tambourine; model skeleton if available

Introduction:
Bounce (run, jump, hop) in and out of others; stop on tambourine.

Shake whole body.
Repeat moving away/towards teacher.
Repeat to music

Development:
On spot to music: nod head, shrug shoulders, bend/stretch elbows/knees, wriggle hips, shake body.
Pupils choose two of above; at tambourine signal, change (phrase A).
Start tucked in, slowly stretch one limb as if escaping from bag; repeat and bring it back in again.

Repeat several times; last time whole body escapes.
Link escape with phrase A. Add bouncy travel.
Practise with music, emphasising the gradual escape, getting the body into action and travelling everywhere.
Discuss how the piece should end; practise. Perform several times.

Conclusion:
Reach up high; curl up small, making one part of the body lead the action.

Tell teacher which body parts were used.

Unit 1, lesson 4 ▷

Theme: Mighty Muscle; contrast of tension	*Resources:* music: *Strong, Heavy, Powerful* from *Technical Tasks* by Barry Bygraves (which can be obtained from Orwell Tapes, Music Services, Bedford); percussion instruments
Purpose: PoS General a4	
Activity bank: Dance: 4	

Introduction:
In space stretched out; tense muscles and make small shape.
One limb after another: punch out; pull back in. Repeat changing level.

From small tight shape, expand and feel lighter, return to tight shape tensing whole body. Repeat.

Development:
Copy teacher doing a pushing action as if moving a heavy object.
Repeat: pupils choose other body parts and levels.
Leap into air as if angry, tense muscles, make strong shape on landing and stamp around.

Make strong shape, breathe out and flop to floor.
Repeat: let one part of the body at a time flop.
Ask pupils what other things muscle people do; ask them to show.
With teacher guidance, link the pushing, stamping, flopping movements and add their own ideas.

Conclusion:
Breathe out and make a small shape; be blown into big shape by breathing in.

Unit 1, lesson 5 ▷

Theme: bubbles; gentle action with contrast of speed	*Resources:* pot of bubble liquid; tambourine; music: *Aquarium* from *Carnival of the Animals* by Camille Saint Saens
Purpose: PoS General a3, a4; c1	
Activity bank: Core: 2, 3; Dance: 3, 5	

Introduction:
Run gently around room; on stop, hover and balance.
Repeat: vary level/direction.

Long steps, placing feet carefully on floor; end by quickly spinning round and then hovering.

Development:
Start hand in front of face, watch it float high into the air, bring it back in.
Repeat: change body part, level of floating and body support.
Flick hands away from body; repeat: use feet, head, whole body; join flicking and floating.

Watch bubbles being blown, floating through the air and bursting.
Copy the action in movement. Link the above: float up, be tossed in the air, settle and burst. Perform to music.

Conclusion:
Get pupils to talk about the actions they did and what they felt like.

Unit 1, lesson 6

Theme: with my teddy bear; focus

Purpose: PoS General a1, a3, a4; b1

Activity bank: Core: 6; Dance: 1

Resources: teddy bear per pupil; music: *Teddy Bears' Picnic*

Introduction:
Creep slowly towards teacher; at signal dash away, look at teacher as you approach.

Put teddy on floor; repeat above using teddy instead of teacher.
Step towards, away from and round teddy (phrase A).

Development:
Learn to skip.
Make a shape from which it is possible to look to one side, the other, up and down, as if searching for something; do this quickly and slowly.
Put teddy on floor and make a 'funny' shape to amuse teddy (phrase B).

Watch examples and ask pupils to tell you why the shape is 'funny', e.g. upside down, body twisted, head between legs, wobbly.
Choose two shapes and join them together.
With teacher guidance, link phrases A and B and finish with everyone skipping round own teddy.

Conclusion:
Sway from one side to another and slowly sink to the floor.

Ask pupils what they think teddy bears do at a picnic.

Unit 1, lesson 7

Theme: teddy bears' picnic

Purpose: PoS General a3, a4

Activity bank: Core: 6

Resources: teddy bear per pupil, music: *Teddy Bears' Picnic;* video *Coppelia* (choreographed by Arthur Saint Leon, available from Dance Books, Cecil Court, St Martin's Lane, London WC2N 4EZ)

Introduction:
Skipping with teddy to end in own space; put teddy on floor; skip round teddy (phrase A).

Development:
Repeat the looking idea from last week; remind about level and direction (phrase B).
Link phrases A and B.
Repeat phrase A and put teddy in middle of room and skip into a space.
Make 'funny' shape to amuse teddy as last week.

Choose two shapes and join them together. (One of the shapes must have the feet higher than the head.) Finish by shaking all over as if laughing.
All pupils skip in circle round the bears, pick up own bear and skip 'home'.
Teacher guides changes throughout. Repeat whole several times.

Conclusion:
Sit on floor and rock teddy to sleep.

Unit 1, lesson 8

Theme: Christmas

Purpose: PoS General a3, a4

Activity bank: Dance: 3

Resources: presents to take to infant Jesus; music: a carol, e.g. *Rocking*

Introduction:
Tiptoe in and out of one another.
Repeat: all going in one direction behind teacher.

Stop at intervals and look up to ceiling; hover/balance as they do this.

Development:
Lie on floor as if asleep; wake up by stretching, i.e. stretch and stretch, stretch to standing, turn around and look for the star, pick up a present to take to Jesus. Follow the star; using the musical phrase: travel a little way, stop and look, look, look. Repeat several times. Last time all look in one direction.
Tiptoe behind teacher who winds around hall and stop as if looking at infant Jesus.

A few at a time creep towards the baby and put present down; using the musical phrase: step, step, step, step, step, step and stop.
Lift present up high and put on floor. Sit down.
Rock gently from side to side. Come to knees.
Raise hands as if in prayer and sink to floor. Repeat many times.

Conclusion:
Sing the carol.

Unit 1, lesson 9

Theme: Christmas (continued)

Purpose: PoS General a1; b1

Activity bank: Dance: 6

Resources: parcels of different shapes and sizes; music: *Jingle Bells*

Introduction:
Lift an imaginary box; carry into a space.
Repeat: change shape of box, body part with which carried, speed at which carried.

Pupils choose one and practise.

Development:
Start closed in; open out right side, open out left side, whizz round and finish closed in. Repeat: use legs.
Use the above to show opening of parcel; remember what shape the parcel was.
Show in movement what was in the box; use all of body, change of speed, tension and level.

In small groups skip as if reindeer pulling a sleigh; make a pile of presents in the middle.
All sit around the parcels. Collect parcel in turn and open. Move in the manner of the present inside (e.g. Thunderbird). Put present on floor; skip round it.
Gradually get smaller and smaller until fall asleep on the floor.

Conclusion:
Gradually stretch out and come up to standing.

Unit 2, lesson 1

Theme: pathway

Purpose: PoS General a3; b2; c1

Activity bank: Core: 6; Dance: 7

Resources: line drawings; paper, crayons/pencils; percussion instruments

Introduction:
Pupils choose one of the shapes from Dance activity 7; walk this shape on the floor.

Repeat: very small, very big, skipping, marching.
Repeat the above with a different shape.

Development:
Draw the shape in the air; change level, body part, body support and speed in turn.
Discuss how the darker parts could be shown in the dance; pupils show this.
Repeat: use other shapes.

Choose one shape to use for the floor pattern and a different one to draw in the air.
Make the darker parts important. Watch another child working and draw on a piece of paper the two shapes he or she made.

Conclusion:
Talk about the things that different shapes remind the children of.

Unit 2, lesson 2

Theme: tick-tock-stop; metric rhythm 4/4

Purpose: PoS General a4; b1; c1

Resources: clock/metronome; drum/claves; music:

Syncopated Clock by Leroy Anderson, *Symphony* by Krystof Penderecki (opening section)

Introduction:
Listen to clock/metronome ticking. On the spot make movements which are like this; use every part of the body.

Show in movement the sound an alarm makes.
Join together the alarm movements and the ticking movements; do this on the spot and in travel.

Development:
Use *Syncopated Clock*. Travel for eight beats, making shapes with the body as they go; make a big change of shape (surprise) and hold for eight beats. Repeat many times.
Repeat: emphasise rhythmic actions to fit the music.
Make big circles which take eight beats; vary body part making circle, like the hands on a clock.

Pupils choose own way of mixing ticking movements and circling movements.
Clap rhythm: 1, 2, 3 and 4 with teacher; stamp it; change body shape.
Perform to music; teacher guides by playing drum/claves.
Link this with circling and being still; teacher guides changes.

Conclusion:
Finish phrase on the floor; slowly sit up and walk to teacher.

Listen to opening section of Penderecki's *Symphony*.
Talk about the movements they have been doing.

Unit 2, lesson 3

Theme: Chinese New Year; rhythm and pathway

Purpose: PoS General a1, a3; b1; c1

Activity bank: Core: 3; Dance: 8

Resources: Story of the Hearth God Tsao-wang (see pp. 17–18); music: *The Story of the Dragon Monster* on *Music for Movement*, BBC PTT324

Introduction:
Practise rhythm from lesson 2 (i.e. 1, 2, 3 & 4) stamping. Revise clapping rhythm.

Add arms waving at sides of body while stamping. Travel behind a partner, keeping in time.

Development:
Rush from one place to another, stopping low near floor, high in the air.
Practise dusting/scrubbing actions.
Rush to one place: dust the ceiling; rush to another: scrub the floor, e.g. rhythm: rush and dust for eight beats; scrub 1, 2, 3 & 4 four times.
Stop; look up for Hearth God's return.

Practise starting low, leap into air and explode; get as high as possible, make legs and arms all move.
Revise travel from introduction.
Gather in procession behind teacher; all travel as if they are dragon; keep rhythm, wave arms.
Discuss with class how dance might end. Practise end.
Perform whole dance several times.

Conclusion:
Sit round teacher and tell the story of the Hearth God Tsao-wang.

Unit 2, lesson 4

Theme: metric rhythm 3/4

Purpose: PoS General a1, a4; b1, b2

Resources: music: *Oom Pah Pah* from the soundtrack of the film *Oliver* by Lionel Bart

Introduction:
Mark rhythm 1, 2, 3 by doing stamp, clap, clap. Repeat with music.

Repeat: clap knees, shoulders etc. Repeat: clap, stamp, stamp.
Bounce rhythm, e.g. bounce, clap, clap.

Development:
Make a body shape near the floor not on feet; clap rhythm on floor four times; clap rhythm in air four times. Repeat with music.
Copy teacher changing method and location of clapping. Continue making own changes. Pupils choose favourite method, practise and remember with music.
Travel with stamping/stepping or bounding, keeping rhythm with music.

Pupils choose favourite variation, practise and remember with music.
Copy teacher: swing one body part in time with rhythm; repeat using different body parts; repeat, adding a turning action. Pupils practise.
Put on music; pupils perform their favourite sections.

Conclusion:
Sit on floor and rock gently in time with the music.

Unit 2, lesson 5

Theme: Freddy Frog's fall; jumping

Purpose: PoS General a1, a3; b1, b2

Activity bank: Core: 4, 5; Dance: 1

Resources: music: *Music for Dance 1*, Side B (19) by Christopher Benstead (available from 42 Lincoln Road, London N2 9DL); video: *Tales of Beatrix Potter* (choreographed by Frederick Ashton, available from Dance Times Book Centre, 45/47 Clerkenwell Green, London EC1R 2SG)

Introduction:
Practise: jumping, hopping, leaping, bouncing from one foot to two and from two feet to one.

Development:
Start in frog-like shape: bent knees, wriggly fingers; big jumps stretching as if getting out of pond, jump and hold for three counts in frog shape (phrase A).
Repeat with music.
Leap gently from one foot to another as if on water lily leaves, balance and drop to ground as if falling into pond (phrase B).

Conclusion:
Sit down and clap 1, 2, 3, making an accent on 1, 2, 3, 1, 2, 3, gradually making sound louder and softer.

Repeat: vary size of spring, body shape, tension and spread.
Repeat with music.

Repeat phrase B, keeping same pathway.
Link phrases A and B.
Practise making different shapes/jumps, very quickly, low near ground.
Pupils choose one of these to show this is the best frog in the pond, but at end fall over again as if into pond.
Link all the above; pupils add end to dance.
Perform with music.

At some time after this lesson show pupils the Jeremy Fisher extract from the video.

Unit 2, lesson 6

Theme: size of action

Purpose: PoS General a3; b2

Resources: None

Introduction:
Travel with very small steps around the room, on tiptoe, stamping.

Development:
On spot, breathe in and grow; breathe out and shrink; make breath audible.
Make growing so big that children travel to another spot. Repeat: make sound.
On spot make body fill all the space; front, side, behind. Gradually come in to as small a space as possible.

Conclusion:
Lie on the floor in big shape. Make a loud noise. Slowly tuck up and let sound get quieter.

Travel with very big steps in and out of each other.
Ask children who might use steps like these. Repeat in character.

Repeat: change shape, speed, body support. Make sound to accompany.
Travel around the room filling all the space, leaping, falling to floor, rolling and whirling up. Make loud sound.
Travel as above, but very small. Make soft sound.
Link the two.

Unit 2, lesson 7

Theme: balloon, linking phrases

Purpose: PoS General a1, a3, a4; c1

Activity bank: Dance: 9

Resources: blown-up balloons, balloons ready to be blown up; tambourine; music: *Snow is Dancing* from *Children's Corner Suite* by Claude Debussy, arranged Tomita.

Introduction:
Start curled up; grow a little bit and shrink, a bit bigger, then as large as possible; imagine being blown up.

Repeat: very gently.
Practise leaping and jumping.

Development:
Watch a blown-up balloon floating. Copy by travelling and settling on the ground.
Watch a balloon bouncing in the air. Copy by bouncing whole body and parts of body; aim for lightness.
Watch a balloon being blown up and released. Copy by

repeating introduction, then whizzing all over the room until teacher signals stop.
Ask what else can happen to a balloon. Pupils show this in movement. With teacher guidance join the above to make a dance about the adventures of a balloon.

Conclusion:
Half class watch the other half and talk about where they could see different parts of the story in the dance.

Unit 2, lesson 8

Theme: *The Magic Drum*; direction and contrast in tension

Purpose: PoS General a1, a3, a4; c1

Activity bank: Core: 4, 5; Dance: 10

Resources: drum/tambour; story: *The Magic Drum* (see p. 18)

Introduction:
March forwards, backwards and sideways. Teacher beats

rhythm on drum; give signal on drum for change of direction (to avoid words).

Development:
Make movements to match sounds given by teacher on drum, e.g. quiet sounds: small movements; swirling sounds: swirling movements, (phrase A).
Repeat lots of times.
Teacher gives drum rhythm, e.g. 1 & 2, 3 & 4; pupils respond by clapping/stamping.
Repeat lots of times, on the spot and in travel. Make

whole body join in the action; keep action earthbound: feet flat on floor.
Add leaps, turns, changes of level; get feeling of energy and vigour (phrase B).
Pupils choose their favourite actions from the above; link phrases A and B.
Repeat lots of times.

Conclusion:
Tell the story of *The Magic Drum*.

Unit 2, lesson 9

Theme: *The Magic Drum* (continued)

Purpose: PoS General a1; b1, b2; c1

Activity bank: Dance: 10

Resources: drum; story: *The Magic Drum* (see p. 18); music: (a) *Ghana: Ancient Ceremonies,* *Songs and Dance Music* by the Donno Drummers, (b) *Dancin' and Drummin'* by Steve Fox (produced by Primrose Studios, 18 Prospect Street, Lancaster); random straight lines (quite short) marked on floor

Introduction:
Travel in and out of the lines, being careful not to cross; use forwards, backwards, sideways, change of level. Remind pupils of stamping and leaping done last week. Perform with music; teacher gives signal on drum for changes.

Development:
Practise phrases made last week; get difference in quality to match sound; try to repeat the actions exactly. Link travel with these phrases and perform with music, listening to drum for signal to change. Remember to give lots of energy: it is a celebration. Practise jumping/hopping/leaping over a line. Pupils choose favourite actions and repeat lots of times.

Ask pupils what happened in the story when the owner of the drum crossed a line. Ask pupils how this could be shown in their dance. Pupils show this in movement. Link travel, first phrase, crossing the line and ending. Perform lots of times with music, teacher giving drum signal for changes.

Conclusion:
Re-tell the story.

LESSON PLANS FOR YEAR 2

Unit 1, lesson 1

Theme: *The Hokey Cokey;* right and left

Purpose: PoS General a4; b1, b2

Resources: tambourine; music: *The Hokey Cokey*

Introduction:
Make circle facing teacher. Skip towards and away; gallop to right and then to left. Repeat: looking towards direction of travel. Keep light and bouncy.

Development:
Shake right arm to the side; shake left arm to the side; shake whole body. Teacher phrases the action, e.g. shake and shake and s h a k e. Repeat: using legs. Repeat: end shake near the floor. Repeat all this using a poking action, i.e. using words of

song: 'In … out: in, out, in, out', then add 'Shake it all about'. From near floor, wind up to standing in line as if a snake. Turn around to right with right arm leading. Practise whole sequence with music; get difference in feel between 'in, out' action and shaking action.

Conclusion:
Stretch up into air with both arms; let right arm flop to the side, then left arm. Kneel on right leg, then on left leg; lie on floor.

Unit 1, lesson 2

Theme: learning a set sequence

Purpose: PoS General a4; b1, b2

Activity bank: Core: 4; Dance: 11

Resources: folk dance steps and music: *Seven Springs* (reproduced on p.19)

Introduction:
Join hands in a circle; walk round to left for 15 steps and stop. Repeat to right.

Jump and land stamping right foot. Repeat to left.

Development:
Jump into the air, land on feet and kneel down on right knee. Repeat to left.
Stretch up into air with both hands, then curl up small, placing right elbow on floor.

Repeat with left elbow, then head.
Repeat jump into the air, land on feet, place elbow on floor.
Learn whole dance; keep rhythm very precise.
Practise lots of times. Perform lots of times.

Conclusion:
Practise *Hokey Cokey* from last week.

At end, sit on floor; stretch up right side, then left side, then both sides.

Unit 1, lesson 3

Theme: Van Gogh's painting *Starry Night*; combining pattern and mood

Purpose: PoS General a1, a3, a4; c1

Resources: Colour print of *Starry Night* by Vincent Van Gogh; music: *Neptune* from *The Planets Suite* by Gustav Holst; tambourine

Introduction:
Travel around the room making S and O patterns on the floor.

Repeat: slowly/quickly, strongly/gently. Give sound accompaniment.

Development:
Look at picture; ask pupils to identify shapes they have been making.
Can they see other shapes? Pupils show you these in their movements, on the spot and in travel.
Show in movement the difference between the darker and the lighter parts of the picture.

Pupils choose their favourite part of the picture and dance it first on the spot and then in travel.
Repeat: adding turns, jumps and changes of level.
Repeat with the *Neptune* music; make movements match the sound.

Conclusion:
Talk with the pupils about what if feels like when they are out on a dark night.

How might they show these feelings in their movements?

Unit 1, lesson 4

Theme: Van Gogh's painting *Starry Night* (continued); combining pattern and mood	*Resources:* colour print of *Starry Night* by Vincent Van Gogh; music: *Neptune* from *The Planets Suite* by Gustav Holst; tambourine
Purpose: PoS General a3, a4; b2; c1	

Introduction:
Show picture to remind pupils of lesson 3's work.
Ask pupils to show some of the movements they did in lesson 3.

Repeat the actions but do them as if very frightened, then as if enjoying themselves.
Add music.

Development:
Look at smoke shape: start low near floor in rounded shape; rise up cautiously into long thin shape, whizz round and tuck up again.
Repeat: shooting up and drifting down.
Ask pupils to tell you how the mood changes. Repeat with music.

Pupils choose either the frightened or the enjoying movements practised in the introduction; practise with music (phrase A).
Make short dance: some pupils perform smoke phrase; others surround them, doing phrase A. Change over.
Repeat lots of times, making the quality changes very clear.

Conclusion:
One half of the class watches the other half. Ask pupils to identify those who look most frightened, who have

the clearest shape, who make a lot of difference between whizzing and drifting.

Unit 1, lesson 5

Theme: Simon says...; working with a partner	*Resources:* percussion instruments
Purpose: PoS General a1, a3; b1, b2	

Introduction:
Play *Simon says* ..., e.g. 'bounce like a ball', 'float like a feather', 'bounce then float' etc.

Development:
Teacher does one action, e.g. shoots into a star shape; pupils copy it afterwards.
Repeat with lots of different movements and qualities; accompany with percussion.
Pupils work in pairs: one makes a movement; the other copies. Make vocal sound while doing the action (phrase A).

In pairs, walk around the room one behind the other; the back one follows exactly where the front one goes; change level.
Give accompaniment with speed change. Change over leader (phrase B).
Link phrases A and B; teacher guides changes with different sounds on percussion.

Conclusion:
Practise *Seven Springs* (lesson 2) with teacher calling instructions.

Practise *Hokey Cokey* (lesson 1).

Unit 1, lesson 6

Theme: *Trainers;* beginning and ending

Purpose: PoS General a4; b2

Activity bank: Core: 2, 3; Dance: 12

Resources: music: *Rhythm Run* (on a cassette entitled *Rhythmic*, available from The Hum-Drum Music Company, Lower Mytholm, Booth, Halifax HX2 6XB); paper and pencils; poem: *Trainers* by Michael Rosen (see p. 20)

Introduction:
Jog on the spot and in travel, making a clear pathway.

Development:
Ask pupils to describe the route from classroom to hall; draw this on paper.
Walk, in the hall, the pattern of this pathway; note beginning and end. Jog along the pathway. Add actions as in introduction; repeat to music.
Show a starting position ready to jog. How does it end? Repeat: get beginning, pathway and end the same every time.

Repeat: knees high/feet kicking up at the back. Add arm action.

Mime action of kicking a ball.
Give phrase: kick and kick and kick and stop. Repeat with music.
Repeat: kick in different directions. Practise kicking so hard that it causes a turn and/or a hop. Add to end of kicking phrase. Repeat lots of times with music.

Conclusion:
Read the poem *Trainers* by Michael Rosen. Ask pupils where the movements they have done today would fit.

Unit 1, lesson 7

Theme: *Trainers* (continued); structuring the response

Purpose: PoS General a1, a4; c1

Activity bank: Dance: 12

Resources: poem: *Trainers* by Michael Rosen (see p. 20); music: *The Power* by Snap; tambour

Introduction:
Jog on the spot for 14 beats and stop.
Repeat: travelling, using pathway from lesson 6.

Development:
In pairs, one following the other, show a pathway which says 'round the house' then 'down the street' then 'to the shops'. Pupils choose one of these and repeat exactly, one following the other. Change over leader. Repeat with music. Remember start and end position; make this the same as your partner (phrase A).

Remember: knees, arms, start and stop.
In pairs jog one behind the other.

Repeat: showing whether happy or angry.
Practise kicking action (lesson 6) to the music. In pairs do this kicking phrase near partner; try to kick at the same time; remember the turn at the end.
Ask pupils to show what they would do, not say, if they kicked a wall; add this to the end of the kicking phrase (phrase B).
Link phrases A and B. Repeat lots of times to music.

Conclusion:
Read the poem *Trainers* again. Pupils describe the actions they did at the end of the kicking phrase.

Unit 1, lesson 8

Theme: Trainers (continued); structuring the response

Purpose: PoS General a3, a4; c1

Activity bank: Dance: 12

Resources: poem: *Trainers* by Michael Rosen (see p. 20); music: *The Power* by Snap; one pair trainers/pumps per pupil

Introduction:
Find partner; practise the jogging phrase from lesson 7 with music.

Remind about pathway, start, finish, mood. Repeat lots of times.
Practise the kicking phrase from lesson 7 with music.

Development:
Ask pupils what they feel like when they find a hole in their trainers. Ask them to show the feeling in their movement.
Sit on floor in a shape so that they can see sole of foot; move head closer to foot as if looking at hole; throw foot away as if disgusted; shake foot away as if laughing.

Repeat in different positions looking to side and behind body. Choose favourite way and repeat lots of times; must have a change of speed and show mood clearly.
Link jogging, kicking and hole phrases; get pupils to link together smoothly.

Conclusion:
Ask pupils how the dance might end; all choose one idea with teacher.

Remind them of poem.

Unit 1, lesson 9

Theme: performing dances learned

Purpose: PoS General b1, b2

Activity bank: Dance: 11, 12

Resources: music and instructions: for *Hokey Cokey* and *Seven Springs* (see p. 19); poem: *Trainers* by Michael Rosen; music: *The Power* by Snap

Introduction:
Find partner; practise jogging phrase with music.

Development:
Go through each section of the *Trainers* dance, i.e. 'jogging', 'kicking' and 'hole' phrases; make actions clear, definite beginnings and endings; make mood obvious.

Add the ending agreed in lesson 8. Practise with music.
Perform whole dance. Teacher reminds about sections; try to get links smooth; be still at beginning and end.
Practise *Seven Springs* with music.
Practise *Hokey Cokey* with music.

Conclusion:
Perform: *Seven Springs, Trainers, Hokey Cokey.*

Unit 2, lesson 1

Theme: one winter's day; selecting ideas to match stimulus

Purpose: PoS General a1, a3, a4; c1

Resources: pictures of snowmen and winter landscapes; hats and scarves; music: *The Snowman* by Howard Blake; percussion

Introduction:
Take a shape near the floor, hands in front of body. Wriggle fingers; watch fingers and move hands around body; use space to side and behind; sometimes stand up and sit down again. Accompany with percussion.

Development:
Repeat the above, travelling as hands move; go sideways and backwards.
Imagine snowflakes are falling. Ask pupils what happens if a wind blows; show in movement.
Jump up and down on the spot as if very cold; slap hands on body; hug body with arms and throw them out again.
Pupils choose their favourite idea, practise with music; let the movements show they are cold.
Start as in introduction, extend into travel, then do own 'cold' movements; finish high. Repeat lots of times.

Conclusion:
From high position sink to the floor, spreading whole body on way down, as if snow covering the ground.

Unit 2, lesson 2

Theme: one winter's day (continued); working with a partner

Purpose: PoS General a3, a4; c1

Resources: hats and scarves; music: *The Snowman* by Howard Blake: percussion

Introduction:
Repeat 'snow falling' movements and 'cold' movements (lesson 1).
Practise to get the difference in quality of the movement.

Development:
Practise linking these two phrases together.
Add the 'snow settling' phrase (conclusion of lesson 1). Repeat several times.
Starting from spread shape near the floor, curl up and roll a little way, as if being made into a snowball; make the snowball grow. Repeat: to music.
Repeat: two pupils come together and make one big snowball. Together the two pupils start to shake, as if with laughter, and skip around as if the snowball had come to life.
Ask pupils what happens to end the dance; show in movement.
Perform whole dance lots of times.

Conclusion:
One half of class watches the other half; they identify pupils who really look as if cold.
Can they tell you what in the movements makes them say this?

35

Unit 2, lesson 3 ▷

Theme: interrupted and continuous flow

Purpose: PoS General a4; b1, b2

Resources: Chinese bells, cymbal, tambour

Introduction:
Start arms high above head; make big circles with hands while sinking to the floor, turning on the way down. Repeat rising; keep the movement flowing. Give one beat on cymbal for each action.

Development:
Start low near floor; gradually rise and travel round the room; hover and swirl down to the floor. Make the action smooth and on-going like a river flowing. Make a definite pathway and remember it (phrase A). On tambour beat, freeze in wide shape; make sharp cracking movements in time to Chinese bells (phrase B). Repeat using only arms and fingers/legs and feet/trunk. Link phrases A and B; make the quality very different. Add to the end a melting action to end on floor as if pool of water. Repeat whole dance lots of times.

Conclusion:
Rise up as if cracking and melt down to the floor.

Unit 2, lesson 4 ▷

Theme: a windy day; movement and stillness, away and towards

Purpose: PoS General a1, a3; b1

Activity bank: Dance: 13

Resources: percussion instruments which can be carried while dancing; poem: *Stocking and Shirt* by James Reeves (see p. 20)

Introduction:
Bounce around the room while carrying and playing a percussion instrument. Half class hold still position while other half dance and play. Change over on teacher command (phrase A).

Development:
Start away from teacher; on command 'Come!' twirl towards teacher and stop in twisted shape; on command 'Away!' swirl away.
Repeat: taking care over spacing.
Repeat: playing instruments while moving.
Divide class into two halves at opposite ends of hall. One half gives command 'Come!' other half twirls towards them; then 'Away!' and they swirl back.
Add movements which say 'Come!' and 'Away!'. Change over (phrase B).
Repeat introduction phrase A in two halves of the room.
Link phrases A and B.

Conclusion:
Read poem *Stocking and Shirt* by James Reeves.

Unit 2, lesson 5

Theme: a windy day (continued); stillness while others work

Purpose: PoS General a3; b2; c1

Activity bank: Dance: 13

Resources: percussion instruments which can be carried while dancing; poem: *Stocking and Shirt* by James Reeves (see p. 20)

Introduction:
Start in shape as if on washing line; let body dance while still looking as if attached to line. Start with small movements, gradually getting bigger. Teacher accompanies with percussion.

Development:
Half class stays attached to line; other half gets blown off, twirls and swirls into one part of the room and stops; then remaining half is blown off and twirls and swirls into another area (phrase A). Repeat: remembering wind blowing and where to go.
Practise 'Come!' 'Away!' phrase (lesson 4, phrase B).
Link phrases A and B. Pupils play percussion while dancing.

Start in a position as if washing caught in a hedge; pull and tug to try to get free; teacher accompanies with percussion; pupils add vocal sound (phrase C).
Link phrases A, B and C. Practise.
End by flying, whirling and twirling everywhere.
Perform whole dance lots of times.

Conclusion:
Get pupils to tell you differences in feeling between twirling and tugging.

Unit 2, lesson 6

Theme: Spring festival; grow, open and scatter

Purpose: PoS General a3, a4; c1

Resources: None

Introduction:
Sitting on the floor, make a fist, watch whole hand open and close.

Repeat: one finger unfurling after another. Repeat: fast/slow.

Development:
Repeat the above: using whole body, sometimes as one piece, sometimes one limb after another.
Fold right side of body across left, then open out to the side. Repeat: on left side, slowly/quickly.
Start closed in; open out and travel to another spot in the room; fold again.

Repeat: very gently/vigorously.
Start closed in; spin to an open position. Repeat.
Each pupil chooses favourite opening, closing and travelling and links together; must have level and speed change. Repeat lots of times.

Conclusion:
One half of class watches the other half, and identifies pupils who show the difference between opening and closing and those who use changes of level and speed.

Unit 2, lesson 7

Theme: Spring festival (continued)

Purpose: PoS General a4; b1; c1

Activity bank: Dance: 14

Resources: pictures of Kathakali hand positions (see p. 21); music: *Homage to Mahatma Ghandi*

Introduction:
Stamp feet on floor with knees slightly bent; seven stamps and stop. Practise placing feet on ground toe before heel, and heel before toe.

Eight heel/toes, then eight big stamps; involve whole body. Perform vigorously as if warming the earth for the seeds (phrase A).

Development:
Learn Kathakali hand shapes from Dance activity 14. Change from one to the other smoothly; look at hands. While sitting, start with one hand to side; trace a big circle above the head to end in shape on the other side. Repeat this, adding 'bud' shape in hands.

Repeat from different starting positions to different ending positions and add travel between.
Try lots of ideas, then choose favourite. Watch hands; keep clear pathway; repeat start and end positions exactly (phrase B).
Perform phrase A, then B, then A again.

Conclusion:
Tell the Hindu story of Holi.

Unit 2, lesson 8

Theme: Spring festival (continued)

Purpose: PoS General a3, a4; b2

Activity bank: Dance: 14

Resources: music: *Homage to Mahatma Ghandi*;

tambourine; video: *Indian Dance 2* (available from Elm Bank Teacher's Centre, Video Studio, Mile Lane, Coventry CV1 2LQ)

Introduction:
Practise heel/toe and stamping actions from lesson 7. Follow teacher in procession around hall, finishing in

one big circle. Perform hand movements (lesson 7). Heel/toe action into own space and sink to floor.

Development:
In own space practise making bonfire. Start low; with flickering actions rise and spread. Begin very small; one body part at a time, gradually involve whole body until leaping into air, then sink again. Repeat lots of times, working for 'flickering' leading into 'leaping flames'.

Practise flickering on its own; practise leaping on its own; make movements flame-like. Repeat whole phrase. Link procession and bonfire. Repeat lots of times.
When leaping at its greatest give tambourine signal; everyone freeze high looking up; hold for count of ten. Repeat whole dance lots of times.

Conclusion:
Re-tell the story of Holi.
Before the next lesson show children the video of two

dances for Holi: one traditional, the other in modern style.

Unit 2, lesson 9

Theme: Spring festival (continued)

Purpose: PoS General a3, a4; b2; c1

Activity bank: Dance: 14

Resources: music: *Homage to Mahatma Ghandi;* tambourine

Introduction:
Practise toe/heel and heel/toe actions of lesson 7.
Sit on floor; make tiny flickering movements with hands, arms, feet, shoulders, heads. Repeat on different supports including feet. Choose a few of these which best make a fire action and repeat several times (phrase A).

Development:
Practise leaping into the air as if a flame; reach up, bounce out of floor as if hot; hold at the end reaching for ceiling (phrase B).
Link phrases A and B; get change of size and quality.
Link procession of lesson 8 with phrase A and then phrase B.

From freeze, spin out, then skip, jump and leap as if going round the bonfire.
Choose two or three of these and repeat (phrase C).
Link procession and phrases A, B and C.
Perform whole dance lots of times, each time making movements clearer; hold starting and ending position.

Conclusion:
Half of class watches the other half; identify features of Holi; identify pupils whose actions look like flames and say why. Say which parts they liked best and why.

39

GYMNASTICS

ABOUT GYMNASTICS

In gymnastics the focus is entirely on the body and as such this activity offers opportunities for physical activity and learning which differ from other areas of the physical education curriculum. Gymnastics offers movement experiences concerned with learning to control and manage the body in a variety of demanding situations. Children can develop their potential for exploration through natural movement if they are challenged and guided in a safe but stimulating environment.

Given the appropriate stimulus and guidance some children will become quite skillful in gymnastics. Owing to the nature of the activity it is essential that gymnastic experience begins in the early school years for those with the potential to succeed. It is important to note however, that developing excellence is not the principle aim of gymnastics as part of the school PE curriculum and the place for coaching the sport to develop excellence lies outside the classroom in extra-curricular clubs.

Gymnastic activity for everyone offers the opportunity to develop general body management and control by improving balance, co-ordination and the range of mobility of the body. The focus of work with young children is essentially about body management and exploring the range of possibilities within one's own limitations of movement. Gymnastics therefore contributes to the development of creativity in youngsters. As children master basic body management however, gymnastics is also about producing quality of movement. There are expectations in terms of level of precision and control of movement. Hence gymnastics offers children an aesthetic experience through movement and the opportunity to develop aesthetic awareness. Gymnastics, as with all the activities within the PE curriculum, offers the opportunity for physical exercise and the development of important social skills in children by guiding them to work co-operatively and safely together in a specialised environment.

Mention should be made of the resources necessary to teach gymnastics in schools. An indoor space which provides enough room for children to move freely and safely is the only essential ingredient. Often the hall which doubles as a dining room is the most suitable space and, providing the teacher ensures that all chairs and tables are stacked safely in a way which will present no possible danger to the children, this area is quite adequate. If the area has a clean, smooth floor it is advisable to have pupils working in bare feet as they move with greater sensitivity on the floor and on apparatus.

With regard to gymnastic equipment, gymnastic mats are necessary for some of the skill work to be covered, though at Key Stage 1 much of the work can be done effectively on the floor rather than on mats. In addition to mats, the most valuable and versatile piece of equipment is the bench or form. If platforms, such as boxes, are available these are useful particularly if they can be split down to relatively low levels. Tressles are also useful. Many primary schools have a climbing frame and this may be used to incorporate and adapt some of the work on to higher apparatus towards the end of Key Stage 1.

There are two important points to note with regard to the use of equipment in lessons. The first is that the equipment should be designed and utilised by the teacher in order to enable progression of movement material from the floor to the apparatus. Equipment such as climbing frames should not be put up in the area and used as an obstacle for the pupils to play on as this does not present the appropriate learning experience for the pupils. The second is that if traditional gymnastic equipment is not available then adapted equipment such as hoops, ropes and chalk lines can provide pupils with stimulus and challenge for some of the appropriate movement material. You will see from the lesson plans that benches and mats are the pieces of equipment most generally used at this Key Stage.

NATIONAL CURRICULUM REQUIREMENTS AT KEY STAGE 1

The following statements from the programme of study (general) are particularly relevant to gymnastics. You will find these developed in the lesson plans that follow.

Pupils should:

a1) be given opportunities to develop a wide range of simple movements in a variety of activities with and without equipment.

a4) be taught to link movements with increasing control to show changes of direction or levels and variations of speed, tension or rhythm.

a5) be helped to recognise and follow safety procedures, including lifting, carrying and moving equipment.

b1) be encouraged to improve to practise and perform simple skills.

b2) be encouraged to improve performance as they work alone and, when ready, in co-operation with a partner.

c1) be given the opportunity to describe what they and others have done in physical education, and how they did it, using simple, functional and aesthetic terms.

d1) be made aware of the changes that happen to their bodies during exercise.

The programme of study (activity specific) for gymnastics is as follows:

Pupils should:

• experience many ways of performing the basic actions of travelling, turning, rolling, jumping, balancing, swinging, climbing and taking weight on hands, both on the floor and using apparatus.

• be given opportunities to practise, adapt and improve their control of individual actions.

• be given opportunities to link together a series of actions both on the floor and using apparatus, and be able to repeat them.

• be taught to carry and position simple apparatus using the correct lifting technique.

It is also important to bear in mind the end of key statements (see page 4) with their emphasis on planning, performing and evaluating.

TEACHING GYMNASTICS AT KEY STAGE 1

The National Curriculum documentation embodies all that we need to do in order to deliver effective gymnastics and the requirements can be interpreted in quite straightforward terms as follows:

1 The programme of study (activity specific) describes *what* the pupils should be involved in doing. This gives a clear outline of the movement material the teacher needs to cover at Key Stage 1.

2 The programme of study (general) relating to gymnastics describes *how* the activities need to be taught and how the pupils should be doing the activities.

3 The end of key stage statements describe the outcome which will be achieved if the content and the process (the what and the how) are appropriate.

The end of key stage statements consist of three strands: planning, performing and evaluating, which must run through all PE work. The performing or doing is central to our work in PE and it is assumed that for the majority of the time the pupils are demonstrating their ability, understanding and knowledge through performing rather than talking about the movement. The planning and evaluating is however far less apparent and it is perhaps more difficult to ensure that

these are being achieved. In addition the non-statutory guidelines give attention to a number of important considerations which should run through all that we do in PE. These include:

• safety considerations
• cross-curricular links
• health-related exercise
• working with others.

You will find that the three strands of the statements of attainment and awareness of the non-statutory guidelines are reflected in the lesson plans for gymnastics and particularly highlighted in the model lessons on pages 43–45.

Teaching the content

The programme of study (activity specific) specifies a number of basic actions. These are: travelling, turning, rolling, jumping, balancing, swinging, climbing and taking weight on hands. These actions can all be grouped into one of two movement themes:

1 Ways of travelling: these can be defined as jumping, rolling, stepping and sliding actions.

2 Ways of balancing: perhaps best approached through ways of moving into and out of balance.

Everything that children should be doing in gymnastics can be encompassed by these two movement themes.

If, within each unit of work, consideration is given to enabling the children to develop a variety of movements, to link movements and to develop and assess the quality of movement the elements within the programmes of study will be adequately addressed. Here is a model for preparing teaching material based on this formula:

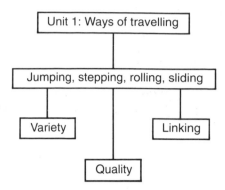

The teaching material set out in the lesson plans that follow provides two units of work, one on ways of travelling and one on ways of balancing, for Reception/Year 1 and two units on the same themes for Year 2. The lesson plans meet National Curriculum requirements in terms of the programme of study (activity specific) by including attention to quality, variety and linking within the themes, as above.

The purpose set out for each lesson demonstrates the way in which the general programmes of study are tied to the units of work. Progression of material has been achieved in a number of ways; sometimes by enabling the pupils to extend the range of moves within a theme (for example, by doing more moves within a sequence) and sometimes by asking the pupils to adapt their movements in a particular way (for example, by making the way of travelling wide or by putting the way of travelling on to the apparatus). Throughout the material provided you will note three key points regarding progression or development of material:

1 The lesson plans on balancing assume that work has been covered on ways of travelling. All of the material utilises this work and is, in effect, a progression from the work on travelling.
2 The material is developed first on the floor and then progressed on to low and or high apparatus.
3 The way in which the movement material is extended is generally by means of varying the shape, the level, the pathway or direction or the speed of the movement. Variety of speed is not actually used at Key Stage 1 as this is a more difficult feature of movement and demands considerable control but it is important to note that change of speed is an important feature of movement work and that reference is made to encouraging pupils to slow movement down in order to improve its quality.

You will find that the Activity Bank for gymnastics illustrates many of the movements and skills which need to be developed at Key Stage 1. Cross-references to these activities are given in the lesson plans.

Covering the statements of attainment and the non-statutory guidance
Reference has already been made to the three strands of the Attainment Target (planning, performing and evaluating) and to the issues addressed in the non-statutory guidance (safety, cross-curricular links, health issues and working with others). You will find these issues reflected in the gymnastics lesson plans and highlighted in the model lessons, but the following general points are made here.

Helping pupils to plan their work
Whenever you tell the pupils to decide which movements to do from a variety of moves which answer the task you are helping the pupils to plan their own work. For example, if you say 'now you decide which part you are going to move on. Which part will you change to when I say change?' in very simple terms the pupils are planning their own work.

Helping pupils to evaluate their own work and that of others
When you draw attention to style, for example if you ask the pupils to 'walk upright' or 'be light on their feet', you are helping pupils to evaluate their own movement. If you ask pupils to watch what someone else is doing and copy them you are helping the pupils to observe the way in which someone else has answered the task and thereby evaluate their movement.

Safety considerations
Safety considerations are very important in the gymnasium. Establish your authority and control initially by doing a very simple activity and ensuring that the pupils are listening and obeying your instructions. The noise level should be such that pupils can always clearly hear the teacher.

Getting out and putting away apparatus must be organised carefully so that pupils are not endangered in any way and so that they gain important life skills such as working co-operatively together, learning regard for one another's safety and learning to lift and place equipment safely.

Here is a suggested routine for getting out benches:

1 Group the pupils into groups of eight.
2 Let one group at a time move to a bench, position/lift and carry it as shown on p. 43. You should be alongside the group to prevent dropping if necessary.
3 Train the pupils to stand and move to a bench on command, and to lift and carry on command.
4 Ensure they place the bench in a space. Try to give the pupils some responsibility here, but adjust if necessary.
5 After placing the bench they should sit on the floor by the apparatus and watch others get out the apparatus.
6 Pupils should all commence work on the apparatus when the teacher instructs them to do so.
7 Reverse the process to put the apparatus away.

Ensure that you use appropriate language to stop pupils when working on apparatus, for example: 'finish off the move you are doing and come down from your apparatus and sit on the floor'.

Cross-curricular links
There is some potential for cross-curricular links in this activity, especially for the development of speaking and listening skills for English. On many occasions the teacher will use subject specific vocabulary which it is essential for pupils to understand, thereby extending the range of pupil's vocabulary. It may be possible to reinforce some of this vocabulary in other areas of the curriculum. The example of body shape has some potential for cross-curricular links in the mathematics area.

The model lessons
Two model lessons have been chosen to highlight general features of teaching that you need to build into all your gymnastics work. You will see that opportunities to plan and evaluate work have been highlighted, together with key points from the non-statutory guidance (safety, working with others, cross-curricular links).

Working with others
Enabling pupils to work effectively with others should not be incidental in your teaching. Part of the potential of the subject is the wealth of opportunity to encourage pupils to co-operate and collaborate effectively. Any time the pupils are involved in evaluating one another's work or in joint planning they are practising important social skills. When they are getting out apparatus and working around apparatus together they are also learning to work effectively with others. On occasions it is appropriate to design phases of your lessons specifically to focus pupils on these skills.

Model lesson 1: Reception/Year 1, unit 1, lesson 3 ▷

Theme: Travelling on large body parts, sliding

Purpose: PoS General a1, a5; b1

Activity bank: Core: 1, 2; Gym: 4a, 4b, 4c, 4d, 4g

Resources: Benches

Activity	Organisation	Teaching points
Introduction: Walk round the room and stop.	Children should be individually in a space.	Ensure attention and response. (!)
Walk and turn.		Children to walk upright, quietly.
Walk towards me.		
Walk away from me.		Ensure use of space.
Run round room.		
Run in and out of each other.		Ensure use of space.
Run. When I clap my hands sit down.		Children light on feet. (EV)
Lie on back. Lie on tummy. Lie on side. What is special about these parts?		Identify body parts. Ensure that they are large body parts.
Development: In a space of your own find a way of moving using one of these parts.	Children sitting on the floor in a space.	
Change to another.		Use pupil demonstration: 'All try what Simon is doing'. (EV)
Now decide which part you are going to move on.		Ask: 'What part are you moving on?'
Which part will you change to when I say change?		Allow children time to decide. (PL)

Get out benches and place in a space.	See remarks on moving equipment, page 42. (!)	
Travel on a large body part along bench.	Have a group near a bench.	Go along bench near you.
Move to another bench.	Ensure use of all space.	No walking or running. Use of space, no queuing.
Travel around room going along and between benches on different body parts.		Change method of travel as they change surface. (PL) Use all benches.
Put away benches.	See remarks on moving equipment, page 42. (!)	

Conclusion:

| 'The mice game' | Children sitting in a space on the floor. | Calm children down and bring them back together. |
| Lie flat on your back, eyes closed, be quite still. When I touch you creep silently to the door. | | Possibly remind children of what they have done. |

Model lesson: Reception/Year 1, unit 1, lesson 7 ▷

Theme: Travelling using different body shapes

Purpose: PoS General a1, a4

Activity bank: Core: 2, 3; Gym: 1i, 1j, 1k, 2d, 2f, 2i, 3a, 3b, 3e, 3f, 4a, 4d, 4e, 4f, 4g

Resources: Benches

Activity	**Organisation**	**Teaching points**
Introduction: Individually travel around the room, moving in and out of one another.	The children should be individually in a space.	Ensure use of space. (!) Look where you are, avoid others. Travel on any body parts.
When I say 'Stop', show me a star shape.		Recap on body shape. (X)
Repeat. On 'stop', show me a pencil shape. Repeat. On 'stop' show me an egg shape.		Encourage stretching fully in shape.
Continue this activity, but make the shape travel: i.e. stop and show a star shape, travel in that shape, stop and show a pencil shape, travel in that shape, etc.		Feed in ideas on ways of travelling. (PL) Holding a shape (see gym bank). Suggest travelling close to the floor.
Development: Travel in and out of one another in a star shape, pencil shape, egg shape.		Allow some time to experiment. (PL) Suggest travelling by rolling or sliding, or on hands and feet, in order to develop a variety of ways.
Look at others in the group. Can you see clearly what shape they are?		Encourage pupils to watch others and check their own body shape. You may want the pupils to give each other feedback. (WWO EV)

44

Get out benches and place in a space.	See remarks on moving equipment, page 42. (!)	
Working on your own bench, travel along in a star shape, pencil shape, egg shape.	A group to each bench.	Pupils to work on the bench they got out.
Look at some of the ideas in the group.		Allow time to experiment and develop ideas, encourage sharing of ideas with others. (WWO PL EV)
Choose one way of travelling in each shape.		This involves use of space and linking skills. Help the pupils by encouraging them to think ahead.
Travel round from bench to bench. Travel in pencil shape on your bench, travel in egg shape across the floor to travel in star shape on next bench you come to.		Which bench are you going to next? How will you change from one shape to another? If someone *is* in your way or crossing your path wait for them to go before continuing. (WWO !)
Put away benches.	See remarks on moving equipment, page 42. (!)	

Conclusion:

Show me an egg shape.	Children individually in a space.	This is designed to calm down and bring to a close.
Very slowly and silently grow into a pencil shape.		Stress the need to be quiet throughout.
Move silently to the door in that shape.		

GYMNASTICS ACTIVITIES BANK

Activity 1: Jumping actions

A jumping action is one where the body is entirely off the ground and in the air for a moment. In all jumping actions:

1 Use arm swing to assist elevation.
2 Ensure the head and chest are up.
3 Ensure good body line, point toes and fingers.
4 Bend knees and ankles to receive weight on landing.

1a: Jump two feet to two feet

1b: Jump one foot to the other foot – a leap

1c: Jump one foot to the same foot – a hop

1d: Jump one foot to two feet – a take-off for flight

1e: Jump two feet to one foot

Jumping actions can be developed by changing bodyshape in the air or changing direction in the air, or by incorporating apparatus.

In all of these actions it is important to:

- prepare by making an arm swing
- make a shape when in the air
- straighten out before landing.

1f: Two feet to two feet – a star jump

1g: Two feet to two feet – a tuck jump

1h: One foot to the other foot – a turning jump

1i: Jumping two feet to two feet on to and off a bench

1j: Jumping one foot to two feet along the bench

1k: Jumping two feet to two feet along the bench

1l: Jumping one foot to the other – leaping along the bench

Jumping actions can be on to different body parts. In all these actions arm swing is very important to give momentum.

1m: Jumping from feet to hands – the bunny jump

1n: Taking the bunny jump on to the bench

1o: Jumping on to bottom on a box top

1p: Jumping on to tummy on a box top

Activity 2: Stepping actions

A stepping action is one where different parts of the body come to the floor in turn, one after another. In these actions:

1 Concentrate on bodyline and tension.
2 Reach for the floor with the next body part.

2a: Crawling tummy down

2b: Crawling tummy up

2c: Rotating from tummy up to tummy down

These action can be developed by taking them across or along apparatus.

2d: Cartwheeling

2e: Crawling along a bench

2f: Crawling over a bench

2g: Cartwheeling over a bench

Stepping actions can be developed by changing bodyparts.

2h: A stepping action with straight legs

2i: A stepping action with legs straddled

2j: A stepping action with body tucked

Activity 3: Rolling actions

A rolling action is one which takes the body over large surfaces and where there is continual contact with the floor. In all rolling actions:

1 Concentrate on body shape. If tucked, keep tight; if stretched, stretch fully.
2 Stress key points for each action as outlined.

47

3a: A pencil roll

3b: An egg roll

3c: A side roll

3d: A circle roll

Rolling actions can be developed to take you along, on to and off apparatus.

3g: A circle roll to come into contact with a bench

3e: A side roll on to a bench

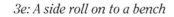

3f: A side roll along a bench

The following two rolls are not rolls which should be specifically taught at key Stage 1 but reference to the correct performance will help if you have pupils who are able to perform these movements.

3h: A forward roll

3i: A backward roll

Activity 4: Sliding actions

A sliding action is one where the body remains supported on the same body part and there is continual contact with the ground. In all sliding actions:

1 Stress bodyline and tension.
2 Ensure attention to body shape: if tucked, ensure body is fully tucked; if stretched, ensure it is fully stretched.

4a: Sliding on back

4b: Sliding on front

4c: Sliding on side

4d: Sliding on bottom

Sliding actions can be developed by changing body shape.

4e: Sliding on back in tucked shape

4f: Sliding in a V shape – legs straddled

Sliding action can also be developed by moving on to or coming off apparatus.

4g: Sliding along a bench on bottom

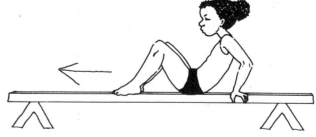

4h: Sliding off a box

49

Activity 5: Balances
A balance is when the body is held still and good bodyline and body tension is maintained. In all balances:

1 Stress pulling away from the point of balance.
2 Stress the importance of the body line – point toes and fingers, keep head up.
3 Stress the importance of body tension, pull everything together.

5a: Body patches

5b: Body points

LESSON PLANS FOR RECEPTION/YEAR 1

Unit 1: Ways of travelling, lesson 1

Theme: travel using feet – running, jumping, skipping

Purpose: PoS General a1, a4; b1

Activity bank: Core: 1, 2, 3, 6; Gym: 1a

Resources: none

Introduction:
Walk round room, stop on command.

Walk towards and away from teacher – use all of the space in the hall.

Development:
Run using the space. Run towards and away from teacher.
Skip in and out of one another.
On the spot, jump from two feet to land on two feet. Do small jumps keeping your feet together so that you are

bouncing round the room like a jumping bean.
Move round the room like a jumping bean.
Link movements: on command from teacher, run, skip, jump.
Run in and out of one another, skip away from teacher, jump towards teacher.

Conclusion:
Stand in a space: back straight, feet together, look at

teacher, be quite still for a moment, walk quietly to the door.

Unit 1: Ways of travelling, lesson 2

Theme: travel on hands and feet – crawling, jumping

Purpose: PoS General a1; b1

Activity bank: Core: 2, 3; Gym: 1m, 2a

Resources: none

Introduction:
Run round the room. Don't touch anyone, stop on

command. Be aware of use of space. Put hands on floor, travel with hands and feet down.

Development:
Feet together: like jumping beans, bounce around the room.
Hands on floor: can you still do a jumping action with feet? – bunny jumps.
Link movements on command: crawl with feet apart, bunny jumps with feet together.

Choose which one to do first, change on command.
Travel round the gym and change the way you travel from crawling to bunny jumps. Use the space by moving in and out of one another.
Think of other ways of travelling, look at what others are doing and share your ideas.

Conclusion:
In a space sit on the floor with legs straight out in front

of you and back straight. Be quite still for a moment, walk quietly to the door.

Unit 1: Ways of travelling, lesson 3

Theme: travel on large body parts; sliding

Purpose: PoS General a1, a5; b1

Activity bank: Core: 1, 2; Gym: 4a, 4b, 4c, 4d, 4g

Resources: benches

Introduction:
Walk round room. Go towards and away from teacher and others. Run, on command stop and lie on tummy, lie on back, sit on bottom, lie on side. Identify body parts as large surfaces.

Development:
Find a way of moving on one of tummy, back, bottom, side – change to another part.
Teacher looks at what the pupils are doing, selects some of the ideas for all the pupils to try.
Choose one way of travelling, choose another, travel using the two ways chosen, change on command.

Take benches out.
Travel on one body part along bench, get to another bench – no walking or running, travel round room and along benches on different body parts.
Put away benches.

Conclusion:
'The mice game'

Lie flat on the floor in a space, lie very still and quiet, when teacher touches you creep silently to the door.

Unit 1: Ways of travelling, lesson 4

Theme: travel on large body parts; sliding and rolling

Purpose: PoS General a1, a5; b1, b2

Activity bank: Gym: 3a, 3b, 4a, 4b, 4c, 4d, 4e, 4f, 4g

Resources: benches

Introduction:
Travel round room on hands and feet.
Travel by sliding on bottom, tummy, back, side – travel towards/away from teacher. Move around with as many parts touching the floor as you can.

Development:
Turn from tummy to back, continue to turn, stretch while you turn. This is a pencil roll.
Tuck tight, turn from tummy to back. This is an egg roll.
Travel round using an egg roll or a pencil roll.

Take benches out.
Slide on benches, roll on floor.
Use different body parts to slide on, use as many benches as you can.
Put away benches.

Conclusion:
As previous lesson, 'The mice game'.

Unit 1: Ways of travelling, lesson 5 ▷

Theme: travel on large body parts; sliding and rolling

Purpose: PoS General a1, a4, a5; b1

Activity bank: Core: 1, 4, 6; Gym: 3a, 3b, 3e, 3f, 4a, 4b, 4c, 4d, 4e, 4f, 4g

Resources: benches

Introduction:
Travel on feet or hands and feet. On command change direction. Travel on feet and link three ways of travelling. Teacher led – jump, skip, step.

Development:
Can you slide or roll in different directions?
Watch some examples. Teacher puts together three movements, pupils copy.
Take benches out.
Show slides and rolls in different directions on apparatus and on the floor.
Look at examples: link a slide and a roll; one move at least should be on apparatus.
Put away benches.

Conclusion:
Stand in a space, shut your eyes tight, stretch as tall as you can, bring arms slowly down to sides, open eyes and walk quietly to the door.

Unit 1: Ways of travelling, lesson 6 ▷

Theme: travelling with attention to body shape – pencil, egg, star

Purpose: PoS General a4; b1, b5

Activity bank: Core: 3; Gym: 2h, 2i, 3a, 3b, 3c, 4a, 4b, 4c, 4e

Resources: None

Introduction:
Travel round room on feet. Stop on command and show a pencil shape, a star shape, an egg shape. Travel round room. On command show one of these shapes of your choice; it should be clear which shape it is.

Development:
Travel by sliding or rolling in a pencil shape.
Travel by sliding or rolling in an egg shape. Look at some examples.
In a space on feet, show a star shape. Make it travel.
Lie on the floor, show a star shape. Can you make it travel?
Look at examples, try some ideas.
Teacher led: travel round room in a star, egg, pencil shape.
Choose one way of travelling in each shape and link star, egg, pencil.

Conclusion:
In a space stand quite still – very slowly stretch out to a star shape and hold it still, then very slowly tuck in to an egg shape. When teacher touches you creep to the door.

Unit 1: Ways of travelling, lesson 7 ▷

Theme: travelling using different body shapes

Purpose: PoS General a1, a4

Activity bank: Core: 2, 3; Gym: 1i, 1j, 1k, 2g, 3a, 3b, 3e, 3f, 4d, 4e, 4f, 4g

Resources: benches

Introduction:
Travel round the room running in and out of one another. On command stop and show me the shape I ask for – star, pencil, egg.
Hold last shape and make it travel.

Development:
Travel using a star, pencil, egg shape – teacher led.
Take benches out.
Travel on a bench in a star shape, in a pencil shape, in an egg shape. Look at some ideas and try them.
Link the three ways of travelling. Begin with a star shape along a bench, then do pencil or egg on the floor to get to another bench, then do third shape along the next bench.
Put away benches.

Conclusion:
In a space on the floor get into an egg shape, be quite still and quiet. Very slowly grow to a pencil shape or a star shape and slowly and silently move to the door in your shape.

Unit 1: Ways of travelling, lesson 8 ▷

Theme: linking ways of travelling by jumping, rolling, sliding

Purpose: PoS General a1, a4, a5; b1

Activity bank: Core: 3, 4; Gym: 1i, 1j, 1k, 1l, 1n, 3a, 3b, 3e, 4a, 4b, 4c, 4d

Resources: benches

Introduction:
Jumping beans – travel round the room bouncing two feet to two feet.
Stop on command, turn to face a different way and go again.
Travel by sliding, on command slide in a different direction.
Travel by rolling, on command roll in a different direction.

Development:
Choose a way of jumping. What shape are you – star or pencil shape?
On command jump around the room, on stop slowly come down to the floor and show a roll or slide along the floor.
Take benches out.
Travel over the bench using a jump.
Travel along the bench using a jump.
Travel to the next bench using a roll or a slide.
Put away benches.

Conclusion:
In a space on the floor, sit up straight with legs out in front. On command tuck tight into an egg shape and hold it still, then very slowly stretch out to long shape and lie flat on the floor and silent. When teacher touches you creep silently to the door.

Unit 1: Ways of travelling, lesson 9

Theme: linking ways of travelling with different body shapes

Purpose: PoS General a1, a4; b2

Activity bank: Gym: 1i, 1j, 1k, 1l, 1n, 3a, 3b, 3c, 3d, 4a, 4b, 4c, 4d, 4g

Resources: benches

Introduction:
Travel round room running. On command change to rolling in pencil shape, sliding in pencil shape, jumping in star shape, rolling in egg shape.
Choose one other way: the shape must be clear.

Development:
Take benches out.
Jump over bench, slide to next bench, jump along bench, roll to first bench and jump over – repeat.
Show a pencil shape, an egg shape, a star shape in those ways of travelling.
Allow time for pupils to select and practise sequence.
Demonstrate sequences.
Put away benches.

Conclusion:
In a space lie quite still. On command, stretch out to a star or a pencil shape, hold stiff and relax, walk quietly to the door.

Unit 2: Ways of balancing, lesson 1

Theme: balancing on large surfaces of the body

Purpose: PoS General a1; b1

Activity bank: Core: 2, 3, 4, 6; Gym: 5a

Resources: none

Introduction:
Run in and out of one another. On command stop perfectly still. Repeat.
Run, jump, skip round the room in and out of one another. On command sit down, lie on back, lie on tummy, lie on side.

Development:
Walk round room. On command choose one of the parts of the body used in the introduction to balance on, take hand and feet off the floor, hold for three seconds.
What is a balance? It is different from just sitting/lying down. You need to pull everything together, feel strong.
On command slide on chosen part of body and turn to balance on another part.
On command roll or slide and balance on body parts I say.
Choose two parts to balance on – teacher led. Balance first, slide and move to balance on second part, slide out of balance.

Conclusion:
Stand in a space, feet together, head up, back straight.
Lift one foot off the floor and try to stand still, stretch away from the floor. Stand up straight again and walk quietly to the door.

Unit 2: Ways of balancing, lesson 2 ▷

Theme: balancing on smaller body parts

Purpose: PoS General a1; b1

Activity bank: Core: 1, 2, 3; Gym: 5b

Resources: none

Introduction:
Run in and out of one another. On command stop perfectly still. Walk in and out of one another. On command balance on bottom, back, tummy, side. Pull everything together to feel strong and steady.

Development:
What other parts of the body can you balance on? Use pupil ideas. All try balancing on two hands and one foot, one hand and one foot, knees and elbows.
Teacher led travel round the room walking, running, jumping. On command balance on three 'points' of the body. Try two 'points'. Stretch away from the floor to show a good balance. Choose one balance you can do well and link to teacher's timing. Walk and on command hold your balance for count of three, after three move off using a jumping action, on command hold your balance for count of three. Repeat sequence of walk to balance, jump to balance.

Conclusion:
As previous week: stand in a space, lift one leg in the air and try to hold it still for a count of three by pulling up through the body. Relax and walk quietly to the door.

Unit 2: Ways of balancing, lesson 3 ▷

Theme: combining balancing on small and large body parts

Purpose: PoS General a1, a4; b2

Activity bank: Core: 2, 3, 4; Gym: 5a, 5b

Resources: none

Introduction:
Run in and out of one another. On command balance on two hands and one foot, two knees and two elbows, one knee and two elbows.

Development:
Choose one balance on three points. Travel by jumping and on the count of three balance on three points. Travel by walking and on the count of three balance on three points. This time from your balance go down to the floor and travel by sliding and on the count of three balance on a large surface or a 'patch'.
Now travel by rolling and balance on a different patch.
Link in teacher's time: jump two, three and balance on three points, slide two, three and balance on a patch, roll two, three and balance on a different patch.

Conclusion:
Standing in a space feet together and back straight, stretch up to tiptoes and slowly go down to the floor and show me one balance on three points. Hold it still and change to one balance on a patch. Stand and walk quietly to the door.

Unit 2: Ways of balancing, lesson 4

Theme: balancing on or against apparatus on large body parts

Purpose: PoS General a1, a4, a5

Activity bank: Core: 3; Gym: 5a

Resources: benches

Introduction:
Travel round the room in any way you choose and on command show me a balance on a patch, on points. Hold the balance still for count of three.

Development:
Take benches out.
Use a bench to balance on a patch. How many patches can you balance on either on or against the bench? Look at some of the pupils' ideas, all try examples.
Linking – teacher led. Travel along the bench by sliding and when I say balance on a patch, hold for three seconds then move to another bench by rolling. When I say balance on a patch on the floor, then slide along the next bench on a different part of the body and balance on a different patch.
Put away benches.

Conclusion:
Sit in a space on the floor, legs straight out in front of you and hands behind and to the side. Keep feet together and try to keep legs straight and lift legs straight out in front of you so that you are like a letter V. Relax, stand and walk quietly to the door.

Unit 2: Ways of balancing, lesson 5

Theme: balancing on large and small body parts on apparatus

Purpose: PoS General a4, a5; b2

Activity bank: Core: 3, 4; Gym: 5b

Resources: benches

Introduction:
Travel by sliding and show me a balance on your tummy, on your bottom, on your side. Travel by jumping and show me a balance on three 'points'.

Development:
Take benches out.
Find ways of balancing on points on the bench or on the floor but touching the bench. Look at pupils' ideas, all try some ideas.
Balance on or against your bench on two or three points and find a way of moving out of that balance to slide along the bench.
Begin away from the bench, jump to the bench to balance on points and slide to balance on a patch, roll to another bench and repeat.
Put away benches.

Conclusion:
Stand in a space on the floor, jump two feet to two feet and go down to crouch. Put hands on the floor and walk hands out away from feet until you are stretched, lift one foot off the floor and hold it still. Stand up straight and walk quietly to the door.

Unit 2: Ways of balancing, lesson 6

Theme: balance with focus on body shape

Purpose: PoS General a4; b1, b2

Activity bank: Core: 1, 3, 4; Gym: 2c, 2e, 2g, 3a, 3b, 3e, 3f, 3g, 5a, 5b

Resources: benches

Introduction:
Travel round the room in a long shape: walking, jumping, rolling or sliding; change way of travelling on command.

Travel in a small shape and change on command.

Development:
Travel in a long shape and show me balances in that long shape. Change the way of travelling. Are there different balances you can do? Travel in a small, tucked shape and show the different ways of balancing.
Choose a small shape to travel in, show me a balance in

the small shape and then from the balance stretch it to a long shape and make it travel. Show a balance in the long shape.
Link, in your own time, travel and balance in a tucked shape, stretch to a long shape, travel and balance in a long shape.

Conclusion:
Stand in a space in a long shape, stretch as long as you

can and step to a wide shape, tuck to a small shape, repeat. Stand and walk quietly to the door.

Unit 2: Ways of balancing, lesson 7

Theme: balancing with attention to body shape on apparatus

Purpose: PoS General a4, a5; b2

Activity bank: Core: 3; Gym: 2e, 2f, 2g, 2i, 2j, 3a, 3b, 3c, 3d, 3f, 4e, 4g, 5a, 5b

Resources: benches

Introduction:
Travel in a pencil roll and on command show me a balance on a patch, on points. Travel in a small shape by

jumping and show me a balance on a patch, on points. Travel in a wide shape. You find a way of balancing on a patch, on points.

Development:
Take benches out.
Travel along a bench in a small, tucked shape and show a balance on a patch, on points.
From one of your balances can you stretch into a long

or wide shape and move to next bench in that shape? Show a balance in a long shape on the next bench. Repeat and allow time to select ideas.
Put away benches.

Conclusion:
Lie in a space on the floor, stretch as long as you can, as

wide as you can. Can you get to your feet in a wide shape? Stand up straight and walk quietly to the door.

Unit 2: Ways of balancing, lesson 8 ▷

Theme: sequencing into and out of balance on apparatus

Purpose: PoS General a4; b2; c1

Activity bank: Core: 3; Gym: 2g, 2h, 2i, 2j, 3a, 3b, 3c, 3d, 3e, 3f, 3g, 5a, 5b

Resources: mats, benches and low platforms

Introduction:
Travel in a wide shape, balance on command, tuck to a small shape and travel and balance, stretch to a long shape and travel and balance.

Development:
Take mats, benches and low platforms out. Arrange as shown in the diagram.

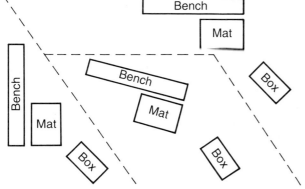

Using apparatus find a way of travelling and balancing in a wide shape.
Allow time to experiment. Use pupil demonstrations to share ideas, then help pupils with the timing by telling them when to travel and balance.
Begin on or near your apparatus in a wide shape; travel, travel, travel and balance and hold. Repeat several times to teacher's timing.
From the balance position now tuck to small shape.
As before, allow time to experiment with travel and balance in small shape.
Put away apparatus.

Conclusion:
In a space sitting on the floor make a wide shape, tuck to a small shape and stretch to a long shape. Stand and walk quietly to the door.

Unit 2: Ways of balancing, lesson 9 ▷

Theme: sequencing into and out of balance on apparatus

Purpose: PoS General a4; b2; c1

Activity bank: Core: 3; Gym: 2g, 2h, 2i, 2j, 3a, 3b, 3c, 3d, 3e, 3f, 3g, 4a, 4b, 4c, 4d, 4e, 4f, 4g, 4h, 5a, 5b

Resources: mats, benches and low platforms

Introduction:
Travel in a wide shape, balance, tuck to a small shape, travel and balance, stretch to a long shape, travel and balance.

Development:
Take mats, benches and low platforms out (see lesson 8). Recap on first part of sequence from lesson 8. Allow time for the pupils to remind themselves of their sequence, give help and guidance. The pupils should have a wide travel to wide balance and then tuck to a small travel to small balance.

Take the group through the sequence before adding stretch to long travel to balance and hold finish.
Look at the sequences, part of the group at a time, tell the pupils watching what to look for and give the pupils performing the timing while they work.
Put away apparatus.

Conclusion:
Sit in a space on the floor – talk about what they have done over the unit of work. Lie flat and play the 'Mice Game'.

LESSON PLANS FOR YEAR 2

Unit 1: Ways of travelling, lesson 1

Theme: travelling on feet with attention to body shape – jumping actions

Purpose: PoS General a1; b1

Activity bank: Core: 1, 4, 5, 6; Gym: 1a, 1b, 1c, 1f, 1g, 1h, 1i, 1j, 1k

Resources: mats and benches

Introduction:
Run around the room in and out of one another. On command change to hopping, skipping, jumping.

Jumping 1, 2, 3 and 4 change to face another way and repeat.

Development:
In a space on the spot, jump from two feet to two feet, stretch in the air, what shape can you make?
Try jumping from one foot to same foot – a hop.
Try jumping from one foot to the other foot – a leap.
Are there other ways of jumping?
Take benches and mats out.
Stand on a bench and try the jumping actions to bring

you off the bench onto the mat. Show me different shapes in the air.
Try the jumping actions along the bench and onto, off, over the bench.
Choose two ways of jumping and travel round the gym jumping over and along the benches showing different shapes.
Put away apparatus.

Conclusion:
Lie in a space on the floor and play the 'Mice Game'.

Unit 1: Ways of travelling, lesson 2

Theme: travelling on hands and feet using stepping actions

Purpose: PoS General a1; b1; c1

Activity bank: Core: 1; Gym: 2a, 2b, 2c, 2d, 2e, 2f, 2g

Resources: benches

Introduction:
Walk round the room, back straight, head up, take long

steps, point toes – step 1, 2, 3, 4 and change to stepping backwards, sideways to both left and right.

Development:
Travel around the room using hands and feet in stepping actions. Look at pupils' ideas. All try travelling by crawling tummy down, crab walk tummy up, cartwheeling idea. Can you do those going feet first, hands first and sideways?

Take benches out
Try different ways of using hands and feet to go along the benches feet first, head first and sideways. Use pupil demonstrations to give a range of ideas.
Put away benches.

Conclusion:
In a space on the floor show a balance on hands and feet.

Can you make this move without putting any other body part on the floor? Stand and walk to the door.

Unit 1: Ways of travelling, lesson 3 ▷

Theme: developing ways of travelling using hands and feet

Purpose: PoS General b1, b2; c1

Activity bank: Gym: 1m, 1n, 2d, 2e, 2f, 2g, 2h, 2i

Resources: mats and benches

Introduction:
In a space, balance on combination of hands and feet. Can you make this travel?
In a crouch position, put hands on the floor and push feet up off the floor, keep knees bent – can you make this move (a bunny hop)?
Using same starting position, now straddle legs. How many ways can you find to move in this position.
Encourage pupils to watch one another to develop ideas.

Development:
Take benches and mats out.
Try to put some of the ways of travelling used in the introduction on to the apparatus.
Try each way of travelling along, over, on and off the apparatus.
Choose two ways of travelling using hands and feet and show each going over and along a bench.

Conclusion:
In a space on the floor, put hands on the floor and straddle legs. Travel to the door making that shape move.

Unit 1: Ways of travelling, lesson 4 ▷

Theme: travelling using larger body parts; rolling – side and circle roll

Purpose: PoS General a1, a4; b1, b2

Activity bank: Core: 2, 3; Gym: 3a, 3b, 3c, 3d, 4a, 4b, 4c, 4d

Resources: none

Introduction:
Run round the room. On command sit down, lie down, lie on tummy, lie on side, each time get up and run again.
From sitting, travel by sliding on bottom, turn to slide on tummy, turn to slide on back.

Development:
Travel by doing a pencil roll, tuck to an egg roll, change on command.
Are there any other rolls you can do? All try a side roll and a circle roll.
Choose two rolls and link them together. Can you put a sliding action in the middle? Roll to slide to roll.

Conclusion:
In a space tuck into a tight ball and try to rock forwards and backwards and side to side. Stand and walk to the door.

Unit 1: Ways of travelling, lesson 5 ▷

Theme: travelling on large body surfaces on apparatus

Purpose: PoS General a1, a4, a5; b2

Activity bank: Gym: 3c, 3d, 3e, 3g, 4g, 4h

Resources: benches, low platforms and mats

Introduction:
Travel round the room by sliding or rolling. On command change the way of travelling. Change and change again.

Development:
Take benches, low platforms and mats out.
On the apparatus try to slide over the top of the bench or platform as well as along.
Choose one rolling action to do on a mat. If you can do a side or a circle roll choose one of those two and do your roll so that it brings you next to a bench or platform. Then slide over or along the apparatus and continue to travel round the gym. I should see a roll to bring you to the bench or platform and a slide over or along.
Put away apparatus.

Conclusion:
In a space lie flat on back and do a pencil roll to finish on your tummy. Push yourself along, feet first then head first on your tummy. Stand and walk to the door.

Unit 1: Ways of travelling, lesson 6 ▷

Theme: travelling using different levels

Purpose: PoS General a4; b1, b2; c1

Activity bank: Core: 2, 4, 5, 6; Gym: 1i, 1j, 1k, 1l, 1n, 2e, 2f, 2g

Resources: benches and low platforms

Introduction:
Travel round the room running, jumping, hopping, skipping, using hands and feet and rolling, sliding. Change on command.

Development:
Take out benches and low platforms.
Travel along or over apparatus using feet only. Remind yourself of the different ways you can travel and choose one way of travelling using feet only.
Travel along and over apparatus using hands and feet. Can you do the cartwheel or the straddle legs travel? Choose one way of travelling using hands and feet.
Link feet travel to hands and feet travel. Repeat so that you know the pattern and direction.
Travel along apparatus using a sliding action. Make this the beginning of your sequence.
Slide to feet travel to hands and feet travel. Look at sequences on the apparatus.
Put away apparatus.

Conclusion:
Lying in a space pencil roll towards each wall in turn, push yourself round on tummy or back to face each direction. Stand and walk to the door.

Unit 1: Ways of travelling, lesson 7

Theme: travelling using different levels

Purpose: PoS General a4; b1, b2; c1

Activity bank: Gym: 1i, 1j, 1k, 1l, 1n, 2e, 2f, 2g, 3c, 3d, 4e, 4f, 4g, 4h

Resources: benches and low platforms

Introduction:
Travel by running in and out of one another, jumping, skipping, hopping.

Travel by a stepping action using feet only then hands and feet.
Travel by rolling or sliding.

Development:
Take out benches and low platforms.
Recap on sequence from lesson 6 – slide to travel feet only to travel hands and feet.
Go to starting position for sliding action, move four steps away from apparatus and work out a way of rolling towards the apparatus and getting into sliding position.

Can you do the circle roll or the side roll? If you can put one of those rolls in to begin your sequence.
Link roll to slide to feet to hands and feet.
Look at sequences and focus pupils' attention to make sure the pupil they watch has the correct sequence of moves.

Conclusion:
Sit straddle legs on the floor. All try a circle roll to face the other wall. Stand and walk to the door.

Unit 1: Ways of travelling, lesson 8

Theme: travelling using different levels and change of direction

Purpose: PoS General a1, a4, a5; b1

Activity bank: Gym: 2d, 2h, 2i

Resources: benches and low platforms

Introduction:
Travel in and out of one another using hands and feet. On command change to travel in a different direction, forwards to backwards to sideways, change and change again.

This time travelling by sliding, change and change again.
Now change the way of travelling and the direction, change and change again.

Development:
Take benches and low platforms out.
Choose one way of travelling from the sequence in lesson 7. Can you make that travel go forwards and backwards and sideways? Try a number of ideas. Use pupil demonstration.

Can you do the straddle hands and feet travel in each direction or can you do the cartwheel in each direction? Choose one way of travelling that you can do and show it travelling forwards, backwards and sideways.

Conclusion:
In a space stand in straddle hands and feet and travel

forward, back, to one side then the other. Stand and walk to the door.

Unit 1: Ways of travelling, lesson 9

Theme: sequencing ways of travelling using different levels and directions

Purpose: PoS General a4; b2; c1

Activity bank: Gym: any from activities 2, 3 and 4

Resources: benches and low platforms

Introduction:
Travel by sliding. Go forward, backward and to sides on command.

Travel by rolling, go to different sides on command.
Travel by hands and feet, go in different directions on command.

Development:
Take out benches and low platforms.
Recap on way of travelling which you could do in different directions.

Link into the sequence of roll to slide to feet to hands and feet (from lesson 7). Show chosen way of travel in different directions.
Look at sequences and focus pupils' attention.

Conclusion:
Sit up straight on the floor, recap on what they have done.

Lie flat and play the 'Mice Game'.

Unit 2: Ways of balancing, lesson 1

Theme: ways of balancing on large body surfaces ('patches')

Purpose: PoS General a1, a2; b1

Activity bank: Core: 2, 3, 4, 5, 6; Gym: 5a

Resources: none

Introduction:
Run in and out of one another. On command stop perfectly still, stretch up away from the floor, repeat.

Vary the travel – skip, jump, hop and stop then stretch away on command.

Development:
Travel using a sliding action and stop and pull away from the floor on command.
Which patch are you on?
Travel with a rolling action, balance on command, which patch are you on?
Choose a slide and balance on command, hold for the

count of three, repeat the action and come to the same balance each time I say 'Stop'.
Choose a roll and balance on command, hold for the count of three, repeat and come to the same balance each time I say 'stop'.
Link to teacher's time – slide to balance and roll to balance, repeat.

Conclusion:
In a space stand up straight on two feet, lift one foot off the floor and hold still.

Can you stretch your leg out in front, behind? Can you stretch your arms out? Relax and walk quietly to the door.

Unit 2: Ways of balancing, lesson 2 ▷

Theme: balancing on small body parts ('points')

Purpose: PoS General b1, b2; c1

Activity bank: Core: 3, 4, 5, 6; Gym: 5b

Resources: none

Introduction:
Travel round room running, skipping, jumping, hopping and stop on command.

Hold still and stretch away from the floor. How many parts of you are on the floor?

Development:
Travel on hands and feet and stop on command. Change travel.
All try a bunny jump. When I say stop try to stay still. How many parts or 'points' are on the floor? Can you make it less? Pull away from the floor. Lift one foot then one hand.

Travel with tummy up and stop on command. Repeat above.
Link travel tummy down then tummy up and stop on command and show a balance. Find different ways of balancing from the travel.

Conclusion:
Stand in a space and stretch up to the ceiling. Can you take one foot off the floor and hold still?

Show a balance on two points, hold it still.
Walk quietly to the door.

Unit 2: Ways of balancing, lesson 3 ▷

Theme: combining and developing balances on points and patches

Purpose: PoS General a1, a2, a3

Activity bank: Core: 2, 3, 4, 5, 6; Gym: 5a, 5b

Resources: benches and/or low platforms, i.e. box tops

Introduction:
Travel round room by running, hopping, skipping, jumping and stop and balance on command.

Travel by rolling, sliding and hands and feet and stop on command.

Development:
Choose a way of rolling or sliding and on command stop and balance. Repeat. Use the same balance each time (you may need to continue to roll after I say 'Stop' until you come to your balance).
Travelling on hands and feet, stop and balance on command. Get as few points on the floor as you can in the balance.

Take benches and/or low platforms out.
Travel to a bench using your rolling action. Show your balance near to the bench.
Travel along the bench or over the bench using a way of travelling on hands and feet. Show your balance as soon as you can after I say 'Stop'. Hold the balance for a count of three and then continue with the roll.

Conclusion:
Lie flat on the floor on your tummy and grow slowly into a balance on three points.

Stand and walk quietly to the door.

Unit 2: Ways of balancing, lesson 4

Theme: developing the range of balances by using apparatus

Purpose: PoS General a1; b1, b2

Activity bank: Core: 3; Gym: 5a, 5b

Resources: benches and low or medium platforms

Introduction:
Travel using hands and feet and on command show a balance on three points, two points, one point or patch.

Development:
Take out benches and low/medium platforms.
Travel to a piece of apparatus and balance on the apparatus on a patch, on three points, on two points.

Continue the sequence travelling to pieces of apparatus by sliding, rolling or on hands and feet and balance on the apparatus as teacher dictates.

Conclusion:
In a space, balance on two hands and one foot, two

hands and one knee, bottom only.
Stand and walk quietly to the door.

Unit 2: Ways of balancing, lesson 5

Theme: balancing with use of different levels on the apparatus

Purpose: PoS General a1, a2; b2

Activity bank: Core: 2, 3, 5, 6; Gym: 5a, 5b

Resources: benches and platforms of assorted height

Introduction:
Travel round feet only, running, skipping, hopping and stop and stretch away from floor and hold still on command.

Travel by rolling, sliding and balance on command.

Development:
Take out benches and low and high platforms.
Travel to a piece of apparatus and balance low on a patch then high on points.
Make the points as few as you can and stretch away from the floor.

What can you hold on to in order to help you to balance on points high?
Link travel to balance low, travel to balance high. Repeat.

Conclusion:
In a space show me a high balance. Gradually shrink to

the floor and show me a low balance.
Stand and walk quietly to the door.

Unit 2: Ways of balancing, lesson 6 ▷

Theme: developing the range of balances with a variety of body shapes

Purpose: PoS General a1, a2

Activity bank: Core: 3; Gym: 5a, 5b

Resources: benches and/or low platforms

Introduction:
Travel round the room in any way you choose, be able to tell me how you are travelling if I ask. On command show a balance in a long or tall shape.

Travel again and on command show a balance in a tucked or low shape.
Travel again and on command show a balance in a wide shape.

Development:
Travel using hands and feet and on command balance in a long shape, in a wide shape, in a tucked shape.
Take out benches and/or low platforms.
Travel along a bench sliding and on command show a long shape balance.

Travel using hands and feet and on command show a tucked shape balance.
Travel by a roll and on command show a wide shape balance.

Conclusion:
In a space, travel slowly on hands and feet and show me a balance which comes from your travel. Repeat. Look at

examples from the group and possibly ask some pupils to show their work.

Unit 2: Ways of balancing, lesson 7 ▷

Theme: travel into balance

Purpose: PoS General a1, a2; b1

Activity bank: Core: 3; Gym: 5a, 5b and any from activities 1 and 4

Resources: benches and/or low platforms

Introduction:
Travel by running and hold in a star balance.
Travel by sliding on bottom and on command hold in a V sitting position by pulling legs and arms up away from

the floor to point towards the teacher. This is a piked seat balance.
Travel by jumping and hold in a one-foot or two-feet balance.

Development:
Run to a balance. Find a way of balancing without too many moves between the run and the balance. Repeat, it should be a points balance.
Slide to a balance. Repeat.

Jump to a balance. Repeat.
Take benches and/or low platforms out.
Travel to the apparatus and show a long shape balance, travel and show a wide shape, travel and show a tuck shape.

Conclusion:
In a space on the floor, lie quite still, be tense, be relaxed and stand and walk quietly to the door.

Unit 2: Ways of balancing, lesson 8 ▷

Theme: travel into balance on apparatus

Purpose: PoS General a1, a2, a3; b1

Activity bank: Core: 3; Gym: 5a, 5b and any from activity 2

Resources: benches and/ or low platforms

Introduction:
Travel on hands and feet and on command show a balance, on one, then two, then three points.

Development:
Take out benches and/or low platforms. Travel to the apparatus and balance on three points, on two points, on one point.

Link your work to show a travel to balance on one, then two, then three points.

Conclusion:
Travel using hands and feet with tummy facing up to the ceiling. On command, stop and show a way of being

on less points. Travel again and on command balance on more points. Stand and walk quietly to the door.

Unit 2: Ways of balancing, lesson 9 ▷

Theme: out of balance on apparatus

Purpose: PoS General a1, a2; b2

Activity bank: Core: 3; Gym: 5a, 5b

Resources: benches and/or low platforms

Introduction:
Travel using a slide, a roll, hands and feet, a jump and

on command show a balance from each of these ways of travelling.

Development:
Take out benches and/or low platforms.
Travel to the apparatus by using one of these methods and find a balance. Now travel in a different way to the next piece of apparatus and find a second balance. Think about how you move out of your balance into your

travel. Practice sequence of travel to balance, travel to balance and show how you get out of balance in to travel.
Show work to other half of the groups. Focus pupils watching to look for interesting or smooth ways of moving from one balance into a travelling action.

Conclusion:
Sit in a space and discuss what has been covered in the unit of work.

Show your favourite balance, hold it still. Why do you like that balance?
Stand and walk quietly to the door.

GAMES AND ATHLETICS

ABOUT GAMES AND ATHLETICS ▶

At Key Stage 1 athletic activities and games can be combined for the purpose of delivery. The skills of running, jumping and throwing are core skills for both activities. In both games and athletics children are encouraged to improve their own potential by increasing the time, length, distance or success rate. At Key Stage 1 both activities concentrate on improving an individual's performance.

Teachers who use this book will naturally come from a range of backgrounds and experiences. However, it is essential that the maturational level of pupils both in terms of skill and personal development is addressed. From the material provided choose an appropriate starting point that will allow children to succeed and that will at the same time provide a challenge for them.

Games in the National Curriculum provide a range of stimulating and exciting educational opportunities. The key feature of playing games is the development of motor skills, hand–eye co-ordination and strategies linked to playing games. Games produce a high degree of physical activity and skills as well as providing children with the opportunity to develop their social skills and mental alertness. For Key Stage 1 pupils, time should be spent on locomotor skills that include chasing, dodging, hopping and jumping. Key aspects of games and athletics have been found to promote sound growth and development through physical activity that also promotes health. At Key Stage 1 the emphasis should be on individual motor control leading to co-operation with other pupils. There is also ample opportunity for children to compete within each unit of work. Making up games is a feature of the latter part of this Key Stage. Within the context of making games children work together to decide on the rules of their game, which include how to stop and start the game, the boundaries of play and how to score.

Playing games in their simplest form is introduced through the lesson plans. Initially, pupils co-operate with each other, both players aiming to score in the same goal. In this situation, a 1 + 1 or 2 + 2 will demonstrate the co-operative nature of the game. Games lead onto a more competitive nature; here the pupils will be aiming at opposing targets. In this situation, a 1 v 1 or 2 v 2 will demonstrate the competitive nature of the game. In certain situations there will be a 3 v 1 game; here the 'attacking' team is larger than the 'defending' team to ensure that the 'attacking' team's passing skills are developed.

There are three types of game: invasion games (e.g. netball, football and hockey), net/court games (e.g. tennis and volleyball) and striking/fielding games (e.g. rounders and cricket). Although these games are modified at Key Stage 1 to meet children's needs, the skills linked to these groups of games may be used.

Clarification of terminology is always important. The following terms, though similar in meaning, imply different levels of skill. 'Retrieving' suggests that the ball is gathered eventually using hands or feet, whereas 'receiving' implies that the ball is controlled immediately, for example, by catching and trapping, therefore the level of skill in this case is much higher.

The major assumption that is made in all of the lesson plans is that games should preferably be outside on a tarmac area or, when appropriate, on a grass area. Firstly, from a safety point of view, when using games equipment, open space is required to ensure that pupils are not in danger from the activities of others. Secondly, skill development can only occur when there is space for children to practise and explore their own capabilities within the tasks set.

In the lesson plans, grids are used. It would be useful to have these as permanent markings. If grids are not marked, then four markers, such as bean bags or quoits, could be used to mark out a square. In certain lessons, the teacher will define the size of the grid. As the units progress this decision is left to the pupils.

Although the use of a wall features in the lesson plans, an upturned bench can be used as a substitute. Permanent playground markings would be ideal, as lines are a feature of most activities. However, chalk or markers used to define lines or areas would suffice. Being able to communicate effectively is essential in controlling safe activity in large outdoor areas, therefore appropriate use should be made of whistle and voice.

In many of the introductory activities pupils are required to move into and around the space using a variety of locomotor skills. Remember that safety aspects are always important in this work and these will be highlighted in the model lessons.

Progressive activity is a feature of all the units of work through the constituent lessons. Constant reinforcement is an essential part of motor development, therefore many activities are repeated in more than one lesson. You will find that the units of work for games and athletics draw heavily on the core movement skills for Key Stage 1 (pp. 5–7) as well as on the bank of activities specifically for games and athletics (pp. 74–79). In the games and athletics bank of activities, descriptions accompanied by illustrations of fundamental activities such as throwing and catching as well as activities designed to develop such fundamentals are provided. The banks therefore aim to provide the teacher with key points for introducing and developing skills within a unit of work.

NATIONAL CURRICULUM REQUIREMENTS AT KEY STAGE 1

The statements from the programme of study (general) that are addressed within the lesson plans for games and athletics are as follows:

Pupils should:

a1 be given opportunities to develop a wide range of simple movements in a variety of activities with and without equipment.

a2 be encouraged to recognise and make up simple rules, and work within them.

a5 be helped to recognise and follow safety procedures, including lifting, carrying and moving equipment.

b1 be encouraged to practise and perform simple skills.

b2 be encouraged to improve performance as they work alone and, when ready, in co-operation with a partner.

c1 be given the opportunity to describe what they and others have done in physical education, and how they did it, using simple functional and aesthetic terms.

d1 be made aware of the changes that happen to their bodies during exercise

The programme of study (activity specific) for games and athletics is as follows:

GAMES
Pupils should:

● experience using a variety of games equipment including, where appropriate, specially designed equipment for pupils with physical disabilities.
● experience, practise and develop a variety of ways of sending, receiving and travelling with a ball.
● experience elements of games play that include chasing, dodging, avoiding and awareness of space and other players.
● be given opportunities to make up and play games with simple rules and objectives, that involve one person and a limited amount of equipment, extended to working with a partner when ready.

ATHLETIC ACTIVITIES
Pupils should:

● experience and be encouraged to take part in running, jumping and throwing activities concentrating on accuracy, speed, height, length and distance.

TEACHING GAMES AND ATHLETICS AT KEY STAGE 1

Within the National Curriculum, programmes of study (activity specific) for games and athletics should provide pupils with a broad, balanced and coherent experience throughout the whole key stage.

There is one Attainment Target within the National Curriculum PE which incorporates the processes of planning, performing and evaluating. Throughout the lesson plans these three processes are addressed as well as the strands of health, safety and working with others. Model lessons are outlined in this section highlighting how these three processes and strands are incorporated into lesson planning. It is hoped that the model lessons will provide examples which can be used to help you expand on the lessons in each unit.

As mentioned in the introduction to this section there are three groups of games: invasion, net/court and striking/fielding. Although at Key Stage 1 pupils do not play these games in the common form, they will be taught common principles and strategies that are related to playing games in this key stage and these will provide a solid foundation for future years.

The first programme of study (activity specific) for games, 'experience using a variety of games equipment including, where appropriate, specially designed equipment for pupils with physical disabilities', is addressed in the units of work at the beginning of the key stage. Here teachers are encouraged to provide pupils in Reception and Year 1 with a variety of equipment, e.g. bean bags, hoops, ropes and quoits, in order that they develop and improve their manual dexterity and hand–eye co-ordination. The units of work presented are flexible and therefore allow for adaptation by the teacher for children with special needs.

The second programme of study (activity specific) for games is concerned with the three skills of travelling, sending and receiving: 'Experience, practise and develop a variety of ways of sending, receiving and travelling with a ball'. These three skills are the basis on which all games are built. The units of work in this section are based on these skills using a variety of equipment. In early years pupils need to repeat the activities with equipment of different shapes, sizes and weights to become competent in sending, receiving and travelling.

The third programme of study (activity specific) deals with locomotive skills related to both games and athletics. Pupils can experience elements of games play which include chasing, dodging, denying and creating space. In order to address this programme of study, the introductory sections of lessons include activities that

70

are aimed at developing these locomotor skills. Such activities are directly linked to the athletics PoS (activity specific) and also involve the health-related aspect of Physical Education.

Finally, the fourth PoS (activity specific) for games is: 'Be given opportunities to make up and play games with simple rules and objectives that involve one person and a limited amount of equipment, extended to working with a partner when ready.' This has been addressed specifically in the units of work towards the end of Key Stage 1. By Year 2 pupils should have a broad vocabulary of skills, with which they are able to make up and play their own games. Initially the games will involve the child working alone, leading to a more complex structure with a partner. In the first instance the teacher should provide the pupils with a precise framework for the game. Pupils will be given more independence in making their own games once they have developed a broad range of physical and social skills. Through individual, partner and small group work, games making is introduced in the third unit of work in Year 2.

There is only one programme of study (activity specific) for athletics, but it is extremely broad and covers a variety of skills: 'Experience and be encouraged to take part in running, jumping and throwing activities, concentrating on accuracy, speed, height, length and distance.' Within the units of work, the introductory sections of the lesson plans concentrate on running, hopping and skipping. In the light of the above programme of study the emphasis for these activities is on speed or distance. Jumping activities are also a feature of the introductory activities. Again, children may be challenged in their jumping activities in terms of height or length. Throwing is an activity that is concentrated on in games, particularly in the development and conclusion sections of the lesson plans. The use of a variety of balls is encouraged. As the level of skill increases so the emphasis is placed more on accuracy, height and distance.

The programmes of study (general) as outlined on p. 4 are concerned with 'how' the activity is taught. This is of particular importance to the teaching of games and athletics. Pupils at Key Stage 1 should be given opportunities to explore their own capabilities as well being guided into discovering a solution to the task set. However, the important concept for teachers to appreciate is that within this task-setting period children should be given key teaching points in order that their level of skill increases.

In order that Games and Athletics in the National Curriculum can be delivered successfully to pupils at Key Stage 1, the following equipment list is considered to be a minimum requirement:

    bean bags
    hoop
    quoits
    ropes
    cones
    multi markers
    large balls – plastic footballs
              – plastic covered foam balls
              – rugby balls (size 3/4)
    medium balls
    small balls – air flow
              – plastic covered sponge balls
    skittles
    canes
    coloured bands/braids.

Whilst accepting that schools may be unable to purchase all this equipment immediately and that the above it is obviously the optimum level that schools may aim to achieve, the majority of activities can be carried out using the equipment already available in the school.

The model lessons
Two model lessons are provided to illustrate planning and evaluating issues. These kind of considerations need to be built into all your work in this area of PE.

Model lesson 1: Year 2, unit 1, lesson 3 ▷

Theme: travelling and controlling the ball

Purpose: PoS General a1, a5; b1; d1

Activity bank: Core: 2, 4, 5, 6; Games/athletics: 17, 23, 24, 28

Resources: large balls, small balls, medium balls

Activity	Organisation	Teaching points
Introduction:		
Pupils choose locomotor activities, e.g. jumping, hopping, skipping etc. Use different pathways. (P PL)	Moving randomly around the area. (!)	Change direction; change shape (PL)
		Choose pupil demonstrations (EV)
Introduce side-step (P)	Whole class activity	Travel in sideways direction.

		Is your breathing faster? (EV H)
Travel using running (P H)	Moving randomly	Introduce a change of speed: fast (sprinting) slow (jogging)

Development:

Using a large ball, choose a way of travelling with hands or feet. (PL)	Pupils moving randomly into spaces changing pathway.	Encourage a change of: direction, speed (PL)
Repeat using a different shaped ball. (PL)		
Practise stopping the ball. (P)	Stop on teacher's command; lead on to choosing when to stop.	How do you stop the ball when travelling with feet? (EV)
		How do you stop the ball when travelling with hands? (EV)
Pupils choose how to travel and then stop the ball. (PL)		If rolling the ball, 'field' it to stop it.
		If dribbling the ball with feet, 'trap' the ball to stop it.
		If bouncing the ball, catch it with hands to stop.
		Try all of the above, which do you find the easiest? (EV)

Conclusion:

Pairs relay. Each partner travels with the ball using the hands. (WWO P)		
Each player travels with the ball out to the line and back, once each.		Ensure that the waiting player controls the ball when collecting it from the incoming player.
Repeat the above using the feet. (P)		
Repeat for a third time.		Which was the fastest method of travelling? (EV)
Decide on the fastest way to travel. Feet/hands? (PL)		

Model lesson 2: Year 2, unit 1, lesson 8 ▷

Theme: throwing and aiming in pairs

Purpose: PoS General b1

Activity bank: Core: 2, 4, 5, 6; Games/athletics: 16

Resources: medium balls, hoops

Activity	Organisation	Teaching points
Introduction: Revise locomotion. Show your teacher what you can do. (PL P)	Move randomly into a space.	Watch for other class members. (!) Encourage change of: direction, pathway, speed. (PL) Highlight good demonstrations. (EV)

Introduce hopscotch. (P)

Whole group activity.
Follow teacher.

Introduce hopscotch by jumping on two feet apart.
Develop into jumping with two feet apart and landing on one foot.
Try to link these two together, jump with two feet, land on the left foot, jump two feet together, land on the right foot.

In pairs, play follow–my–leader. (WWO)

Label pupils A and B.
A leads, B follows

Swap over after 30 seconds

Encourage a change of:
pathway, speed and direction. (PL)

Leader links together different locomotor skills. (P PL)

Development:
In pairs using medium size ball. Roll ball away from the line, partner runs to receive it. (P ¹)

Swap over after each roll.

Repeat the above, bouncing the ball away from the line. (P)

Change over after each turn.

Partners face each other.

Four metres between each player.

All pairs rolling the ball in the same direction.

Person A rolls ball for partner B to walk towards and receive. (P)

Change over after each turn.
Increase the distance apart with confidence and skill development.

Repeat the above for bouncing.

Increase the speed of the roll/bounce, encouraging the partner towards the ball.

Challenge your partner: send the ball to your partner's side. (PL P)

Which side is it most difficult for your partner to receive the ball? (EV)

Conclusion:
In pairs. (WWO)
Both players stand behind a line.
Two hoops are set out, one close to the line, the other further away.

Take it in turns to bounce the ball into the hoops. (P)

Aim to bounce the ball into a hoop of your choice. (PL)

Aim to bounce the ball into the hoop stipulated by partner. (PL)

How many times do you get the ball into the correct hoop? (EV)

Make up a game that involves bouncing the ball and aiming it into the hoops. (WWO PL)

Think of a rule and how to score a point (PL)
Demonstrate your game to another group. (EV)
Describe to the other group how you score a point in your game. (EV)

GAMES AND ATHLETICS ACTIVITY BANK

Activity 1: Heading a ball

Track ball through air. Move feet to align ball with forehead. Keep knees bent. Stiffen neck ready for impact, extend legs at knees and make contact with centre of ball with forehead. Aim ball forward and high.

Progress from soft foam balls to harder balls.

Activity 2: Hitting ball with hockey stick

Ensure correct grip on stick (left hand on top and right hand on bottom). Hit ball with flat side of stick. Use larger balls initially, progressing on to smaller balls. Control backswing of stick to go no higher than shoulder height.

Activity 3: Sending the beanbag

The illustration shows an example of sending the beanbag to a partner in space. Partner retrieves or catches.

Activity 4: Sending and receiving the football

Place your non-kicking foot by the side of the ball. Take your kicking foot backwards, and then swing forwards kicking through the middle of the ball with instep or toes. Try kicking below the mid-line of the ball, see what happens.

Activity 5: Trapping the football

Partner rolls ball towards you. Track ball carefully. Trap ball in one of two ways:

a) Put foot on top of slowly moving ball

b) Turn sideways on and trap ball with instep. Bend knees before contact with ball to help absorb impact of faster moving ball. Suck the ball into your foot.

Activity 6: Retrieving the rolling oval ball

Partner rolls ball along floor to you. Receiver tracks bobbling ball carefully. Can you roll it so that it doesn't bobble?

Activity 7: Individual hitting skills

Using one soft foam ball and bat 'keep the kettle boiling' (keep batting the ball up as many times as you can). Keep the ball up, when palm is up, or when palm is down. Can you balance the ball on the bat? Can you roll it around on the bat surface? Hit high and low. Hit alternately palm up then down. Walk around (egg and spoon). Walk around whilst hitting the ball in the air.

Activity 8: Throwing and catching

Use a variety of methods for throwing and catching, sitting, standing, throw with left catch with right. Throw ball in air, let it bounce and then catch. Throw ball in air, let it bounce, then control with feet.

Activity 9: Rolling the small ball

Ball in hand, take throwing arm back from the shoulder. Keep palm up, bend legs to get closer to the ground. Swing arm forward and release ball at a point level with the floor.

Activity 10: Rolling larger ball

May need to hold the ball in two hands. Bend knees, lean forward and roll the ball.

Activity 11: Knocking down skittles

The aim of the game is to get children to stand behind the throwing line, and try and knock over skittles/markers. Can be extended into a team game (fastest team wins etc.).

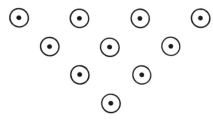

Activity 12: Aiming at goal

'Gate' markers are used to roll, kick, throw the ball between. As children become more successful you may narrow the goals, to make the task more difficult. The task may also be varied to meet the needs of a wider group of people.

Activity 13: Zig-zag relay

Using markers, run in and out of markers. Start behind line, finish over same line. This activity organisation can be used for running, hopping, skipping, carrying a ball, dribbling a hockey/football/basketball etc.

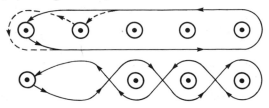

Activity 14: Out and back relay

Start behind line, run out around the marker cone and return. Repeat using different implements or methods or locomotion as in Activity 13.

Activity 15: Running and jumping in and out of hoops

Children run around hoops, jump into hoops, jump out of hoops, jump over hoops. Jump from one foot to one foot, two feet to two feet, one foot to two feet, two feet to one foot etc. Jump for height and jump for distance.

Activity 16: Hopscotch

More than one hoop may be used to initiate hopscotch type activities. A larger number of chalk circles (squares) may also be marked on the playground floor as shown in the diagram.

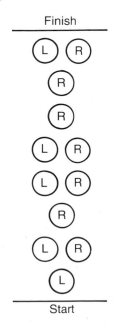

Activity 17: Changing pathway

Changing direction does not involve turning your shoulders, unless combined with a change of pathway. Walking forwards, backwards, sideways whilst always facing the same way means a change of direction. Turning corners, walking in circles, figures of eight, etc. means a change of pathway. The diagram represents walking backwards (this involves a change of direction), turning to the left, walking forward (a change of pathway) and turning to the right then walking forward again.

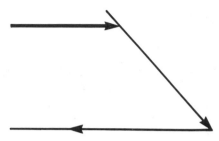

Activity 18: Individual skipping activities

a) Just swing rope around either side of body using one hand only (not jumping over it). When rope hits floor child should take a little jump to find rhythm.

b) Start with rope behind. Turn rope over slowly, and jump once. Then try twice, then three times and so on.

Activity 19: Group skipping activities

Mark an X on the floor where jumper should aim to land. Gently swing rope back and forth under feet only, ask child to jump the rope. Progress on to full circles over head. Try and keep on X. How many can you do? Can you get more than one child in at a time?

Activity 20: Targets

Both circular and square targets may be used on the playground floor or on a wall. If marked on a wall, they should be set at different heights to cater for the ability range within the school. The circle diameter should be approximately 0.75 m as should the width of the square. The centre of each target should range between 1.2 m and 2.0 m above the ground. The circles may be used for aiming beanbags, quoits etc. into. If on the floor, they may be used for bouncing balls into accurately. They may also be used to stand in as discus and shot put

activity circles. On the wall they may be used for ball throwing accuracy and distance when combined with a starting line which may be marked between two and five metres away from the wall.

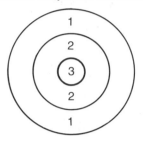 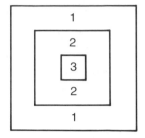

Actiity 21: Hitting a ball

Stand side on to travelling ball. Take bat back very early in the swing. Point to ball with non-hitting hand, then bring bat forward fast to make contact with the ball. Stay relaxed. Try hitting ball upwards and downwards.

Activity 22: Retrieving a rolling/bouncing ball

One person in pair rolls/bounces the ball out, partner retrieves. Increase speed the ball travels at. Adjust size of the ball to your individual needs.

Activity 23: Trapping ball using feet or leg

Watch ball carefully as in Activity 5. This time trap ball with lower leg by bending knee down toward and over the ball. Trap the ball using the outside of the foot.

Activity 24: Throwing and catching (individual)

a) Bounce ball on floor and try and catch.

b) Throw ball/beanbag/quoit up in air and catch. Progress by increasing height or making the ball smaller and harder.

c) Throw from left hand to right hand and back again.

d) This can be repeated using hand hitting instead of throwing and catching.

Activity 25: Kicking

The immature phase

It is noticeable that in the immature phase, the leg tends to just kick at the ball, with very little follow through. There is also little help in kicking from the arms or trunk.

The intermediate phase

In the intermediate phase the child learns to bring the leg backwards in the preparation phase, keeping the leg bent until contact with the ball has been made.

The mature phase

During the mature phase the arm on the kicking side moves backward whilst the other arm moves forward. The movement of the kicking leg starts at the hip, with the non-kicking leg slightly bent at the knee. The leg swings through a long arc, toe is pointed on contact

with the ball, after which the leg has a long follow through, at which point the non-kicking foot rises up onto its toes.

Activity 26: Throwing

The immature phase

In the immature phase there is very little movement of the trunk or legs, the action comes mainly from the arm. The arm action is in fact a pushing action from the elbow, and the follow through tends to be downward and forward.

The intermediate phase

During the intermediate phase, the arm prepares to throw by moving sideways, upwards and backwards, to a point where the ball is almost behind the head, at the same time the trunk rotates backwards. As the throw starts, the arm moves forward in a high position and the trunk moves backward on the non-throwing side. The forceful action of the arm causes the foot on the throwing side to step forward, as the wrist follows through propelling the ball forward and downward.

The mature phase

In the mature phase the arm is taken back as above, the throwing shoulder drops as the trunk rotates backwards taking the weight on to the back foot in the preparation phase. Then as the throw begins the hips rotate leading the shoulders, the elbow leads the wrist, and the weight moves from back to front. The thumb rotates downwards on release of the ball with the fingers being noticeably together.

77

Activity 27: Catching

The immature phase

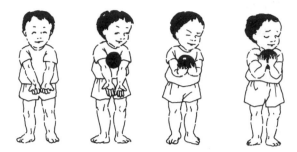

As the ball moves toward the child there is an initial avoidance reaction noted in the turning away of the head or the protection of the face with the arms. The arms at this stage are straight at the elbow, and there is limited movement until the ball makes contact. The child then attempts to scoop the ball into the chest. There is very little use of the hands in this stage of catching. The catch is inevitably poorly timed.

The intermediate phase

Avoidance reaction improves, with eyes closing when contact with the ball is made. At this stage the arms are held slightly bent in front of the body, and initial contact is attempted with the hands. The ball is still however scooped into the chest. Hands are held opposite to each other, fingers point toward the ball. The closing of the hands around the ball is poorly timed.

The mature phase

There is no avoidance reaction. The eyes follow the ball until contact is made. Fingers also point toward ball, and arms give on contact. Arms adjust position to flight of ball, and hands are cupped. The catch is well timed and hands clasp around ball on contact.

Activity 28: Fielding

As the ball is travelling towards the fielder, ensure that the whole of the body is in line with the ball, i.e. the body is directly behind the ball. The body position should be close to the ground, ensuring that the hands are as close to the ground as possible. The hands should be cupped and together in order that the ball does not travel through them. Additionally, the hands should be behind the ball at all times with the fingers pointing towards the ground. Heels should be together and behind the hands.

It is important that the weight and size of the ball is chosen carefully to ensure that the child feels confident in fielding it.

Activity 29: Striking

It is essential that whatever implement is used, the body position is always sideways on to the ball when striking it. This allows lateral swinging of the arms, i.e. from back to front. A backswing is essential for striking the ball, however the greater the backswing, the higher the directional error. It is important to discourage children at this stage from exaggerating their backswing.

The primary function of striking is to hit the ball, sometimes for direction, at other times for distance. It is therefore important that the size and weight of the ball is suitable for the level of skill of the children. A larger, lighter ball is easier to see and thus easier to strike.

Activity 30: 'Stuck in the mud'

One or two children are the catchers. They chase after other members of the class. When the catchers are close to somebody they 'tick' them on the arm/shoulder, after which the person caught stands still with their legs apart, i.e. they are 'stuck in the mud'. As well as trying to avoid the catchers, members of the class can crawl in between the legs of those 'stuck in the mud' in order to release them. After a couple of minutes change the 'catchers'.

Children must be aware of the safety aspects, and should be aware of other group members as they run around the space.

Activity 31: 'Statues game'

In pairs, label 'A' and 'B'. A stands still whilst B runs in and out of the 'statues', i.e. the other members of the class standing still. On the command given by the teacher, B stops still, looks for their partner, and finds the quickest way of getting back to them. Change roles and repeat.

Children should be made aware of the rest of the class, taking care when moving randomly around the area.

Activity 32: 'Tag game'

In pairs, one person is 'on'. They chase after their partner and 'tick' them when they are close by. The other person is then the chaser. The game is repeated. This game should be played for about three or four minutes.

To vary this simple tag game, a bean bag may be carried by the 'chaser' and placed lightly on the shoulder of the partner when close by.

Children should be conscious of others as they move around the area at random. Also, if the game is played with a bean bag, the chaser should place the bean bag on the shoulder of their partner, the bean bag should not be thrown.

Activity 33: 'Cat and Mouse'

In pairs, each player tucks a coloured braid/band in their waistband, to hang down the back of their shorts or skirt. They face each other, and without making any physical contact, they each attempt to get the coloured band out of their partner's waistband. After each successful attempt, the band/braid is returned to the partner and the successful player gains a point. The game is repeated for about five minutes.

Activity 34: 'Dodgeball'

In a group of four or five (the numbers can be more or less, however, children must be active in order that they have a number of attempts), make a circle with one person in the middle. With a foam ball, players on the outside roll the ball aiming to hit the player in the middle on the ankles. The player in the middle moves in order to avoid the ball. They count how many times they were caught on the ankles, i.e. below the knee. After thirty seconds the player in the middle changes.

Children must be made aware of safety; the ball must be *rolled* at the player in the middle, and should not be raised above the knee!

Activity 35: 'The Journey'

The teacher makes up a story that involves the whole class taking a 'journey'. For example:
'Running through the trees (weave in and out of the trees), suddenly, a tiger chases after you (run quickly to avoid the tiger). Then you come to a stream (jump over the stream), then you have to crawl through a tunnel (hands and knees through the tunnel). After running some way the road starts to incline (run as though you are running uphill), then there is a steep hill downwards', etc.

Continue this for about five minutes to ensure that the pupils' heart rates are raised.

Activity 36: Skipping rhymes

a) Hipperty hop to the candy shop,
   To buy a stick of candy,
   One for you,
   One for me,
   One for sister Sandie.

b) Two, four, six, eight,
   Johnny saw a rattlesnake,
   Eating cake by a lake,
   Two, four, six, eight.

c) Jack be nimble,
   Jack be quick,
   Jack jump over,
   The candlestick.

d) I like coffee,
   I like tea,
   I like … (child's name)
   In with me (skips in).

   I hate coffee
   I hate tea,
   I don't like … (child's name)
   In with me (skips out).

e) Cowboy Joe from Mexico,
   Hands up,
   Stick 'em up,
   And out you go!

f) Polly in the kitchen,
   Doin' a bit of stichin',
   In comes a bogey man,
   And out she goes.

g) Two little sausages,
   Frying in the pan,
   One got burnt,
   And the other said 'Scram!'

Activity 37: Dribbling a ball

a) Football
Dribble the ball around the markers. Try and keep the ball as close to your feet as possible. Try and use both the outside and inside of your feet.

b) Hockey ball
Dribble the ball around the markers with your hockey stick. Keep the ball as close to your stick as possible at all times.

c) Basketball
Dribble the ball around the markers. Push the ball hard into the ground in a spring-like fashion, use your fingers to control the ball.

Activity 38: The 'bean game'

Children move around an area specified by the teacher. The teacher calls out instructions from the following list and the children change their method of moving according to the instructions:

Runner bean – run around in and out of other pupils
Jumping bean – jump around in and out of other pupils
Frozen bean – pupils stand still
Chilli bean – run quickly on the spot
Broad bean – make a wide shape and move around the space
Jelly bean – make the body jelly-like
Baked bean – lie on the floor and bake in the sun.

LESSON PLANS FOR RECEPTION/YEAR 1

Symbols on artwork
Note the following symbols are used on artwork throughout the Games and Athletics lesson plans:

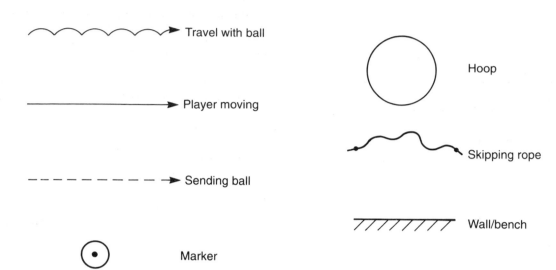

~~~~~~~~→ Travel with ball

————————→ Player moving

– – – – – – → Sending ball

⊙ Marker

◯ Hoop

Skipping rope

/ / / / / / / / Wall/bench

Unit 1: Introduction to small games equipment, lesson 1

Theme: running games

Purpose: PoS General a1, a5; b2; d1

Activity bank: Core: 1, 2, 3

Resources: 10 markers

Introduction:
Children walk around the room/work area. Use commands 'Stop/Go'.

Use of eyes to look where you are going. Be aware of others/equipment.

Development:
March like soldiers. Emphasise higher knee lift, punchy use of arms. Add change of pathway.
Repeat for running. Run with baby steps, run with giant steps, run quietly, run quickly, run slowly.
Use markers. Children run around markers changing pathway. Run in shape of letter S, P, G etc.

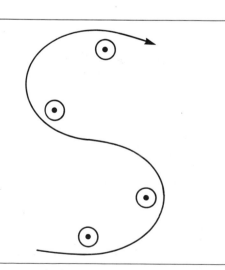

Conclusion:
Run around 10 markers, count them as you go. What happens to your body. Do you breathe faster after exercise?

Unit 1: Introduction to small games equipment, lesson 2 ▷

Theme: jumping games

Purpose: PoS General a1, a5; b2; d1

Activity bank: Core: 4; Games/athletics: 15

Resources: one hoop per pupil (or use chalk circles)

Introduction:
Reinforce walking and running from Lesson 1 in the introductory activities.

Introduce the hoop. Put it in a space. Then walk/run/change pathway around the hoop.
Use 'Stop' and 'Go' commands.

Development:
Introduce hoop or chalk circles with jumping skills and activities.
Step into hoop and out of.
Jump from two feet to two feet into hoop and out of it.

Clock game: jump across circle to make 6 o'clock etc.

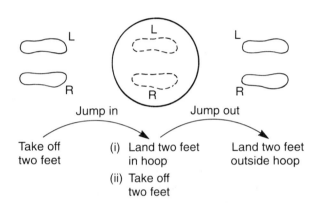

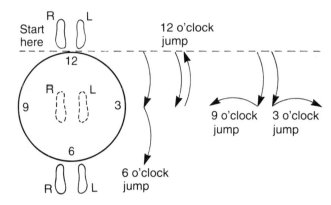

Run around hoop, on clap of hands jump into hoop, then out.
Develop one foot to other, two feet to two feet, one foot to two feet. Develop height and distance.

Conclusions:
Travel in and out of hoop with jumps.
Does your heart beat faster when you exercise?

Unit 1: Introduction to small games equipment, lesson 3 ▷

Theme: jumping and skipping

Purpose: PoS General a1, a5; b2; d1

Activity bank: Core: 6; Games/athletics: 18

Resources: one skipping rope per pupil

Introduction:
Reinforce running and jumping activities from Lesson 2.

Introduce use of ropes. Walk on rope, around rope, over rope. Use variety of shapes with rope, e.g. circle, square, snake or diamond shapes.

Development:
Now develop basic jumping skills using ropes, and then

move on to skipping. Teach progression for skipping as in Games/Athletics activity 18.

Conclusion:
Show what you can do with your rope.
Do you feel warmer after you have skipped?

Unit 1: Introduction to small games equipment, lesson 4 ▷

Theme: bean bags

Activity bank: Games/athletics: 3, 26

Purpose: PoS General b1; c1

Resources: one bean bag per pupil

Introduction:
Walking, running and jumping activities, movement into space.

Stop on command.
Change from running, jumping or walking to a different method of moving on command.

Development:
Running with bean bag. Pick up/put down.
Toss bean bag from one hand to the other.
Slide bean bag with each hand.

Repeat using different parts of the body.
Throw bean bag forward, retrieve.
Throw bean bag sideways, retrieve.

Conclusion:
Find different ways of moving bean bag around the hall/play area.

Swap (change colour) bean bag with friend, keep on moving.

Unit 1: Introduction to small games equipment, lesson 5 ▷

Theme: quoits

Activity bank: Core: 5, 6

Purpose: PoS General b1; c1

Resources: one quoit per pupil

Introduction:
Hop on right foot, left foot, hop and step.
Develop skipping. Skip and change pathway.

Development:
Roll quoit away and chase.
Roll quoit away with other hand. Which is easiest?
Pass the quoit around the body. Which parts can you take it around?

Can you balance the quoit on your head, now move. Can you balance on another body part? Which is the easiest body part to carry it on?
Slide the quoit. Does sliding or rolling make the quoit travel further?

Conclusion:
Travel around the room with the quoit. On command put the quoit down, then pick it up again.

Come together, with teacher review what was done in the lesson.

Unit 1: Introduction to small games equipment, lesson 6 ▷

Theme: foam balls

Purpose: PoS General b1; c1

Activity bank: Core: 1, 2; Games/athletics: 10, 20, 24a, 24b, 24c, 28

Resources: one medium or large foam ball per pupil

Introduction:
Walking, running, change speed on command. Side step to the right and then to the left.

Development:
Carry ball on hands, balance on different parts of the body.
Send with hands and feet. Roll, bounce.

Travel with the ball using hands, feet or other body parts.
Aim ball forward, to hit target on the wall.
Throw ball high and catch.

Conclusion:
Take the ball around the work area to all different parts of the room.
Change ways of travelling.
Move around obstacles with foam balls.

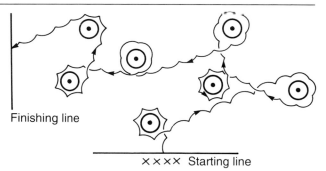

Finishing line

×××× Starting line

Unit 1: Introduction to small games equipment, lesson 7 ▷

Theme: combining activities

Purpose: PoS General b1; c1

Activity bank: Core: 2, 3; Games/athletics: 38

Resources: hoops, bean bags, quoits, markers, skipping ropes, foam balls

Introduction:
Play the 'bean game' (see Games/Athletics activity 38). Start with 'runner bean'. Move on to 'jumping bean'.

Use the 'frozen bean' command to make the children stop and stand still.

Development:
Roll the hoop and quoit – which rolls the furthest?
Slide the bean bag and roll the ball – which moves the furthest?

Roll the ball along a line, can you keep it straight?
Aim bean bags into hoops.
In pairs, bounce ball into hoop, partner B retrieves.
A aims ball at target on wall, partner B retrieves.

Conclusion:
Travel with ball around the hoops/obstacles. On

command, take ball to a specified obstacle, e.g. red hoop, yellow skittle.

Unit 1: Introduction to small games equipment, lesson 8 ▷

Theme: developing partner work and basic hitting skills

Purpose: PoS General b1, b2; c1

Activity bank: Core: 3; Games/athletics: 3, 9

Resources: bean bags, markers, balls

Introduction:
Shadow a partner around a room/space. Stop. Can you touch them with your hand? Vary pathways/speed/ methods of travelling. Swap over.
Keep your eyes on your partner and beware of others.

Development:
Copy a partner rolling a ball in different ways.
Repeat using different ways of throwing a bean bag.
Choose a bean bag or a ball. Slide it to each other. Roll it to each other.
Sit legs astride facing each other and roll back and forth.
Try hitting ball with front/back/left/right hand.

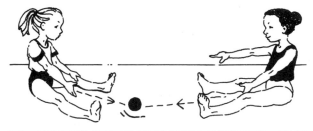

Hit ball between two markers (a 'gate'). Control and hit it back to partner.

A – – – – – – – – – – –▶ B

Conclusion:
Find a number of ways of rolling the ball through the gate to your partner.

Unit 1: Introduction to small games equipment, lesson 9 ▷

Theme: multi-activity

Purpose: PoS General b1, b2; c1

Activity bank: Core: see whole bank; Games/athletics: see whole bank

Resources: hoops, bean bags, quoits, markers, skipping ropes, balls

Introduction:
With a partner, find a number of ways of moving around the space/room.

Choose some equipment to carry around the work area. Change your piece of equipment.

Development:
Show your partner what you can do with a ball/quoit/hoop/bean bag/skipping rope. Can your partner copy you? Swap over.

Develop comparisons between pieces of equipment.
Practise different ways of sending and receiving with a partner.

Conclusion:
Challenge a partner to a skill: jumping, skipping, throwing, rolling, bean bag/quoit/ball etc.

Unit 2: Travelling and sending, lesson 1 ▷

Theme: travelling, and sending using feet

Purpose: PoS General a1, a5; b2; d1

Activity bank: Core: 3; Games/athletics: 4, 5

Resources: one large foam ball per pupil; set of markers

Introduction:
Play the 'bus station' game. In pairs, start at a central marker and lead your partner to one of the four stations set out (e.g. red, yellow, blue, green marker cone). Partner A pretends to be a bus of a certain colour, partner B follows, e.g. red bus to red station (marker). Change over, A follows B, e.g. blue bus to blue station etc.
Visit all stations.

Development:
Travel with large ball using feet. Use one foot, then the other foot. Change pathway etc.

Stop on command.
Send ball to rebound off wall, retrieve.

Conclusion:
Dribbling the ball, travel to four different stations in the work area, as in introduction. Choose your own route. Which is the quickest way?

Unit 2: Travelling and sending, lesson 2 ▷

Theme: developing travelling with ball at feet; sending in pairs

Purpose: PoS General a1, a5; b2; d1

Activity bank: Core 3, 6; Games/athletics: 12, 37a

Resources: one large ball per pupil; one set of markers

Introduction:
Running, skipping etc, around work area. Pretend you are driving a train/car. Play the 'traffic light' game.

Teacher uses colours as commands to control the speed of the children: green for go, amber to slow down, red and amber to go faster, red to stop.

Development:
Travel with large ball. Change pathway. Use any part of feet, especially inside and outside. Which is the best to use to keep the ball close to your foot? Travel with changes in speed. Dribble along chalk lines etc.
Work in pairs. Send ball using feet between markers, partner retrieves and sends back. How many successes can you score?
Make gate smaller and repeat.

A
sends

B
retrieves
then sends
back

Conclusion:
Play the 'traffic light' game whilst dribbling ball.

Unit 2: Travelling and sending, lesson 3 ▷

Theme: developing control with feet; developing accuracy when sending

Purpose: PoS General a1, a5; b2; d1

Activity bank: Games/athletics: 12, 37a

Resources: one medium ball per pupil; one set of markers

Introduction:
'Ghost ball': pretend that you have a ball just in front of your feet and that you are travelling with it around the work area.

Development:
'Stickyball': now get a real ball and repeat, imagine that you are dribbling your ball in a sea of sticky glue. Using medium size ball, travel with ball. Change feet. Dribble forwards/sideways, changing direction. Which is the best part of the foot to use when moving sideways? Work in pairs. Send ball through gate to partner (make gate smaller with greater success). Partner receives and sends back.

Conclusion:
Have a relay race. Work in pairs, A goes first, B goes second. A starts behind line dribbles ball out to marker, stops it, turns and dribbles back, kicks ball to wall, aiming through gate for goal, then retrieves and dribbles back behind line. B then repeats.

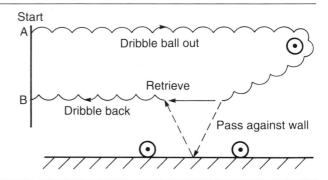

Unit 2: Travelling and sending, lesson 4 ▷

Theme: travelling and sending with hands

Purpose: PoS General b1; c1

Activity bank: Core: 1, 2, 3; Games/athletics: 10, 32, 37c

Resources: one medium ball per pupil; one set of markers

Introduction:
Play the 'tag game' (see Games/Athletics activity 32) walking/running.

Development:
Dribble medium-sized ball with hands in and out of obstacles. Use right, left, front and back of hands; which is the best way?
Roll ball along line (chalk). Roll ball away from yourself, and then retrieve. Roll ball into a space and retrieve.
Work in pairs, roll ball against wall, partner receives. Roll ball between cones, partner receives.

Conclusion:
Play one of these skittle games: 'Ten green bottles' – set up the skittles as shown below. Each partner has five attempts to hit as many bottles as possible.
'Bottle neck game' – set up the skittles as shown below. Each partner has five attempts to get best score in one shot.

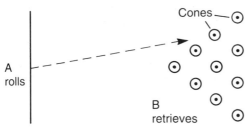

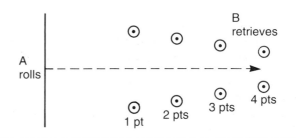

Unit 2: Travelling and sending, lesson 5 ▷

Theme: catching, bouncing and rolling using small balls

Purpose: PoS General b1; c1

Activity bank: Core: 4, 5; Games/athletics: 8, 9, 22, 28, 32

Introduction:
'Bouncy tag': play simple tag 'see Games/Athletics activity 32) using hopping and two-footed jumping to travel around.

Resources: one airflow ball per pupil; set of markers, quoits and hoops – one per pair

Development:
Using an airflow ball, stand in a stationary position, toss ball and catch to start. Roll ball away and retrieve. Bounce ball and clap, then retrieve.
Bounce ball and chase into a new space. Throw ball against wall.
Work in pairs. Aim ball to land in hoop, then partner retrieves.
Bounce the ball to the side, one side then the other.

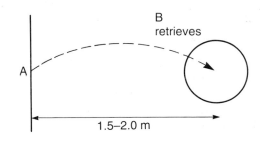

Conclusion:
Play 'Fishies in dishies'. Place quoits or upside-down markers (dishes) at random around the work area. Players start behind line. On command, each tries to find an empty dish to place their ball in, then runs back to starting position.

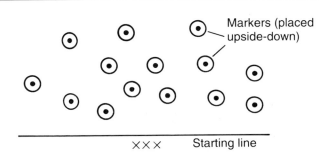

Unit 2: Travelling and sending, lesson 6 ▷

Theme: rolling, bouncing and carrying an egg-shaped ball

Purpose: PoS General b1; c1

Activity bank: Games/Athletics: 6, 9, 10

Introduction:
Working in pairs, have a quoit relay. Partner A runs out, puts quoit down and returns. Partner B run out, picks up quoit and returns.

Resources: one quoit per pair, one hoop per pair; one small oval ball per pupil; variety of round balls

Development:
Carry large ball/egg-shaped ball into a space without using hands (under arm etc.).
Change pathway, change direction – sideways. Put ball down, look around, then pick it up. Bounce ball and chase into a new space.

Work in pairs. Bounce ball into hoop, partner retrieves. Still working in pairs, place ball in quoit, partner picks up. Roll ball away, partner chases and picks up.

Conclusion:
Run and change ball with a person who has a different sized/shaped ball.

Unit 2: Travelling and sending, lesson 7 ▷

Theme: partner work, rolling, bouncing, retrieving; paired relays

Purpose: PoS General b1; c1

Activity bank: Core: 1, 2, 4, 5, 6; Games/athletics: 14, 16, 22a

Resources: one medium round ball per pupil

Introduction:
Revise different ways of travelling.

Develop hopscotch.

Development:
Carry medium-size ball around the work area, in any way you can.
Repeat, but now share your ball with a partner.
Roll ball to partner.
Roll ball away from partner. Partner retrieves.

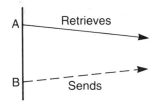

Bounce ball to partner.
Bounce ball away from partner. Partner retrieves.
Repeat, but sender runs to meet retriever.

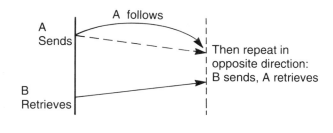

Conclusion:
Working in pairs, have a shuttle relay. A goes first, then B repeats. Run out, place ball in quoit. Run around marker, back to quoit. Pick up ball and bring back.

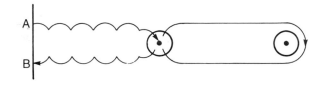

Unit 2: Travelling and sending, lesson 8 ▷

Theme: developing throwing and aiming in pairs

Purpose: PoS General b1, b2; c1

Activity bank: Games/athletics: 8, 14, 26

Resources: chalk circle or hoop per pair; medium size round balls or airflow balls; cones and canes

Introduction:
Work in pairs.
Partner A stands still, partner B circles them.

Side-step facing in toward centre of circle, side-step facing out, which one is harder?
Repeat, this time changing speed.

Development:
Work with partner. Aim ball into hoop (target), partner retrieves.
Aim ball over line/rope, partner retrieves.
Send ball under (use hands/feet)/over (use hands) cane, partner retrieves.

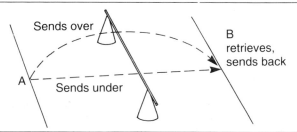

Conclusion:
Have a shuttle relay in pairs. Carry ball out using hands or feet. Send ball under cane. Crawl under cane, jump over it or go around it. Carry ball to line. Return around outside.
Partner repeats.

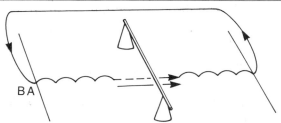

Unit 2: Travelling and sending, lesson 9

Theme: individual sending and receiving

Purpose: PoS General b1, b2; c1

Activity bank: Core: 4; Games/athletics: 4, 5, 6, 8, 9, 10, 15, 22a, 25a, 25b, 25c, 25d

Resources: one hoop per pupil; various balls, enough for one per pupil

Introduction:
Play 'Toad in the hole'. Walk, then run, around hoops placed in work area. On command (e.g. whistle), return to hoop and step into it. Repeat, except this time run around the hoop and then jump into it.

Repeat, but run around hoop, then jump in and land on two feet. Jump out.
Do not jump into same hoop at the same time as someone else.

Development:
Work in pairs, with one ball each. Use hands/feet to carry ball around hoops in work area as shown.

Partners A and B swap balls. Decide how to give them/send them/receive them.

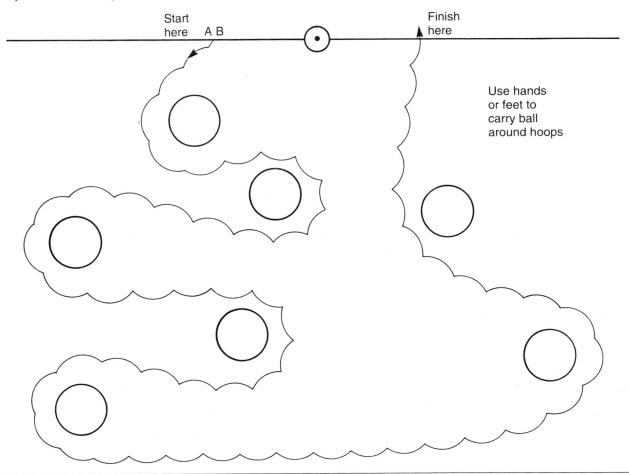

Start here   A B

Finish here

Use hands or feet to carry ball around hoops

Conclusions:
Place hoops around the work area in a snake shape. In pairs, bounce ball into hoop, partner retrieves. Choose free hoops, as you move around work area. Can you bounce ball high and low? Can you bounce the ball then catch it?

Unit 3: Sending and receiving, lesson 1 ▷

Theme: roll and control

Purpose: PoS General a1, a5; b1; d1

Activity bank: Core: 1, 3; Games/athletics: 23, 37a

Resources: one round ball per pupil

Introduction:
'Scarecrows': Walk around, stop on command. Have arms out to sides, bent at elbow. Run, stop, repeat as before with one foot slightly off floor. Repeat, take other foot off floor to balance.

Development:
Dribble large ball using feet. Use one foot then the other, then carry between both feet. Which way lets you move most quickly?
Roll ball away with feet, chase after, then stop with hands. Roll ball away with hands, then run after and stop with feet. Roll ball away using feet, run after stop with feet.
Repeat into space. Which is the easiest way to control the ball?

Conclusion:
In pairs, have a relay. A rolls ball away along a straight line, chases after it, stops it with hands, carries it back to start and gives ball to B. B repeats.

Unit 3: Sending and receiving, lesson 2 ▷

Theme: foot and ball control

Purpose: PoS General a1, a5; b2; d1

Activity bank: Core: 3; Games/athletics: 4, 5, 25, 37a

Resources: one ball per pupil; one set of markers

Introduction:
Dribble ball around obstacle course (made up of markers). Use right foot, then left foot. How many obstacles can you dribble around?

Development:
Dribble with right foot, left foot, inside of foot, outside of foot. Stop with left, right foot. Which foot is it easiest to stop the ball with?
Kick ball, chase after and stop the ball. Kick ball against wall/bench, and stop the ball.
Stop, turn/dribble etc.

Conclusion:
Follow a partner whilst dribbling. Take your partner on an interesting journey around the work area. A leads B, then B leads A.

Unit 3: Sending and receiving, lesson 3 ▷

Theme: hand and ball control

Purpose: PoS General a1, a5; b2; d1

Activity bank: Games/athletics: 24a

Resources: one medium ball per pupil; one hoop per pupil

Introduction:
Run around with ball. Stop on command, use two hands to bounce ball onto floor, then catch or retrieve.

Development:
Run around, get to a line, use two hands to bounce the ball on the line. Run again, stop, bounce twice on a different line. Use two hands, 'bounce ball high, bounce ball low, bounce in the middle and away we go'. Try bouncing the ball as many times as you can without stopping. How many did you do?

Conclusion:
Bounce ball whilst walking around your hoop. Bounce the ball into and then out of the hoop. Try bouncing with one hand. Try a different ball.

Unit 3: Sending and receiving, lesson 4 ▷

Theme: bouncing and catching

Purpose: PoS General b1; c1

Activity bank: Core: 1; Games/athletics: 24a, 24b, 24c

Resources: one ball per pupil

Introduction:
Try bounce/catch, bounce/catch whilst walking along a line (use two hands).

Development:
Throw ball away/bounce and retrieve. Throw high, let the ball bounce, and then 'make a basket' using your hands to catch or retrieve. Concentrate on catching. How may times can you catch the ball in a row?

Conclusion:
Half the class of children stand as 'statues' in the work area. The other half take it in turns to bounce ball around statues. Stop on command. Swap over.

Unit 3: Sending and receiving, lesson 5 ▷

Theme: bouncing, catching and hitting

Purpose: PoS General b1; c1

Activity bank: Core: 3; Games/athletics: 7, 24d, 27

Resources: one ball per pupil: make various size balls available

Introduction:
Running around the work area, bounce the ball once (using two hands) on as many different lines as you can.

How many lines did you bounce the ball on?
Repeat, bounce the ball twice consecutively, on as many lines as you can.

Development:
Pat ball on hand, keep in air. Keep palm up. Try different size balls, do they feel different?

Pat ball on floor using one hand.
Use right hand, use left hand. Pat ball high and low. Is it easier to pat ball high or low?

Conclusion:
How many times can you pat the ball in the air ($\times 1$, $\times 2$, $\times 3$)?

Pat the ball on the floor ($\times 1$, $\times 2$, $\times 3$).

Unit 3: Sending and receiving, lesson 6 ▷

Theme: batting and patting

Purpose: PoS General b1; c1

Activity bank: Games/athletics: 7, 24d

Resources: one bat, one medium ball per pupil

Introduction:
In pairs, play the 'egg and spoon' game. Use medium size ball, balanced on a bat. Take your partner on an interesting journey around the work area. A leads B, then B leads A.

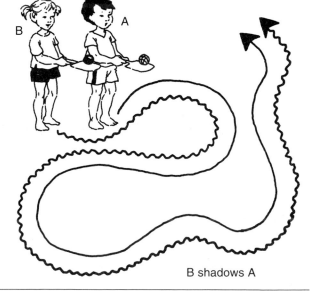

B shadows A

Development:
Using small bats, remain stationary and bat ball up and down on to floor.
Now try and keep it up in the air.

Repeat whilst moving. Move forward, sideways. Change pathway.
Pat ball against a wall. Retrieve.

Conclusion:
Have a relay in pairs. A runs out and round marker carrying a ball on the bat, then returns. B repeats.

Finally, A runs patting ball down to ground and B repeats.

Unit 3: Sending and receiving, lesson 7 ▷

Theme: partner work and rolling

Purpose: PoS General b1; c1

Activity bank: Core: 3; Games/athletics: 5, 6, 9, 10, 22

Resources: one ball per pair: make various size balls available

Introduction:
Play 'Mirror tag'. Follow your partner around the work area. On the 'Stop' command, copy your partner's body shape.

Development:
Work in pairs. Roll ball to partner, stop with hands. (Increase distance between partners, decrease size of ball, or do both to increase difficulty).

Roll ball to partner, stop with feet.
Roll ball to partner's right side, then to left side. Stop with hands or feet as appropriate.

Conclusion:
Roll ball through markers to left or right of partner. How may balls can you roll past your partner? Partner may use hands or feet to stop.

Roll ball to left and right sides

Unit 3: Sending and receiving, lesson 8 ▷

Theme: partner work and bouncing

Purpose: PoS General b1, b2; c1

Activity bank: Core: 1, 2, 3, 4, 5, 6; Games/athletics: 22

Resources: one medium size ball per pair

Introduction:
Play 'Shadow tag'. Work in pairs. Follow and copy your partner's every move around the work area. Stop and swap over.
How fast is your heart beating?

Development:
Work in pairs. Bounce medium size ball to partner. Stop the ball using hands.

Catch ball after one bounce. Throw underarm upwards. Then try overhead downwards. Bounce ball to the side, partner catches.

Conclusion:
Try and roll or bounce the ball past your partner. How many times did you get the ball past your partner? How did you get it past your partner?

Unit 3: Sending and receiving, lesson 9

Theme: partner work, dribbling and hitting

Purpose: PoS General b1, b2; c1

Activity bank: Core: 1; Games/Athletics: 7, 22, 37c

Resources: one bat and ball per pupil; one set of markers

Introduction:
Use medium size ball. Dribble ball around the work area using two hands, then one hand.

Work in pairs. Take your partner for a walk in the country/town (whilst dribbling the ball). A leads B, then B leads A.

Development:
Repeat above using a bat and ball.
Now roll ball along floor to partner using a bat. Partner

stops ball and rolls back with bat. Roll to left then to right. Which side of the bat are you using?

Conclusion:
Try to keep rolling ball back and forth between partners.

Use two markers, roll ball between them. How many times can you do it?

LESSON PLANS FOR YEAR 2

Unit 1: Travelling, sending and receiving, lesson 1

Theme: bean bag, quoit and hoop activities

Purpose: PoS General a1, a5; b1; d1

Activity bank: Core: 3, 4, 5, 6; Games/athletics 17

Resources: bean bags, quoits, hoops

Introduction:
Pupils choose locomotor activities, i.e. walking, running, jumping, hopping, skipping. Stop/start,

change pathway.
Do you feel warm?

Development:
From the bean bags, quoits and hoops, choose a piece of equipment.

Travel with it, change pathway.
Pick it up, put it down, run round it.
Change piece of equipment.

Conclusion:
Work in pairs, both partners have the same piece of equipment.
A shows B how they travel with the equipment. Swap over.

Play the 'Shadow' game, partner follows. Take turns at leading.
Change piece of equipment and repeat the above.

Unit 1: Travelling, sending and receiving, lesson 2 ▷

Theme: hoop and rope activities

Purpose: PoS General a1, a5; b2; d1

Activity bank: Core: 2, 6; Games/athletics: 15, 17, 18

Resources: ropes, hoops

Introduction:
Choose locomotor activities as in lesson 1.

Stop/start, change pathway.
Does your heart beat faster?

Development:
Place ropes and hoop on the floor as shown.

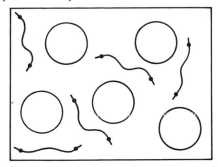

Run around.
Run around, jumping into/over the ropes and hoops.
How many can you jump over in one minute?
Can you jump from one foot to the other, two feet to two feet, one foot to two feet?
Can you imagine that there is a wall around the hoop/rope? Jump as high as you can to get over it.

Conclusion:
Choose a rope or a hoop. Can you skip with it?
Change the piece of equipment.

Practise skipping, begin on the spot, jumping on two feet together or one foot then the other.
Repeat the above, but this time on the move.

Unit 1: Travelling, sending and receiving, lesson 3 ▷

Theme: travelling and controlling the ball

Purpose: PoS General a1, a5; b1; d1

Activity bank: Games/athletics: 14, 17, 23

Resources: large balls, small balls, medium balls

Introduction:
Pupils choose locomotor activities.
Change direction – sideways/backward/forward.

Change speed, i.e. fast and slow.
Introduce side-step.
Is your breathing faster?

Development:
Using a large ball, choose a way of travelling with hands/feet.
Change direction.
Change speed.

Try a different sized ball. Repeat the above.
Practise stopping with the ball.
Travel and then stop the ball, e.g. if rolling the ball then 'field' it.

Conclusion:
Working in pairs, have a relay. Travel with the ball using the hands, out to the line and back, partner then controls the ball and goes to the line and back.

Repeat using the feet.
Repeat deciding on the fastest way to travel.
Which was the fastest way to travel?

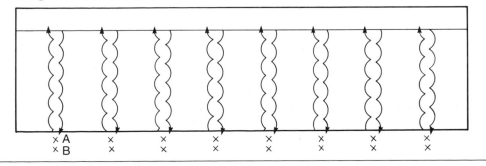

Unit 1: Travelling, sending and receiving, lesson 4 ▷

Theme: development of rolling and stopping the ball using the hands

Purpose: PoS General b2

Activity bank: Games/athletics 22, 28, 32, 34

Resources: small balls, medium balls, markers, foam balls

Introduction:
Play simple 'tag' games in pairs (see Games/athletics activity 32).

Development:
Work alone using a medium/small ball. Roll ball into a space, chase after it and retrieve.
Repeat, sending the ball to the side and backwards.
In pairs: roll ball to a partner, as fast as you can.
How fast can you send it?

Roll ball against a wall for partner to receive on the rebound.
Roll ball between four markers (three gates).

Conclusion:
In pairs: roll ball between the four markers (as above).

In a competitive situation, find a way of getting the ball past partner.
If successful the player has one point.
How many times did you get the ball past your partner?
Increase the number of markers for progression.

Play 'dodgeball' (see Games/athletics activity 34) in groups of six. Five children form the circle, one stands in the middle. Use a foam ball. Aim to hit the feet of the middle person by rolling the ball. After 30 seconds change person in the middle.

96

Unit 1: Travelling, sending and receiving, lesson 5 ▷

Theme: travelling, sending and receiving using the feet

Purpose: PoS General b2

Activity bank: Games/athletics: 12, 18, 23, 25

Resources: skipping ropes, large ball, markers

Introduction:
Work alone: skipping with a rope, staying on the spot.

Try two-footed jumps, one-footed jumps, hopping and stepping. Try forwards and backwards.

Development:
Travel with a large ball using your feet.
Send ball against a wall, retrieve. Use right foot, then left foot.
Which is the easiest?

Work in pairs. Use two markers. Send ball to partner between the two markers. Partner retrieves then sends back. Pupils vary distance between the markers as well as their distance from the markers.
Travel up to the markers then pass ball to partner.

Conclusion:
In pairs: A stands in between the two markers.

B runs around the outside of the two markers with the ball (at feet).
At a suitable point, B passes to A.
A controls the ball and then passes back to B who is running around the markers.
Repeat, changing positions after five circuits each.
Can you send and receive the ball fives times keeping control?

Unit 1: Travelling, sending and receiving, lesson 6 ▷

Theme: patting and catching balls

Purpose: PoS General b1

Activity bank: Games/athletics 7, 18, 24d

Resources: skipping ropes, medium balls, small balls

Introduction:
Skip with a rope, using more advanced skills if possible.

Development:
Work alone using a medium/small ball. Keep the ball in the air using hands.

Pat the ball in the air remaining stationary. (Hand flat and fingers together.)
How many times can you pat the ball without it hitting the floor?

Choose your favourite hand to pat the ball with.
Repeat whilst walking around, leading on to running.
Use the right hand, then the left hand.
Pat the ball on the floor, whilst stationary.

Pat the ball on the floor, walking, leading to running.
Use the right hand, then the left hand.

Conclusion:
In pairs: 1 + 1 co-operation with your partner.
Pat ball in air for partner to catch. Repeat three times, then swap over.

Pat ball on floor for partner to catch. Repeat three times then swap over.

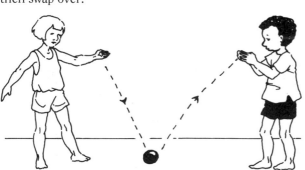

Use alternate hands to pat the ball.
Which is the easiest?
Pat ball to partner. Allow the ball to bounce at first then progress to keeping it in the air.

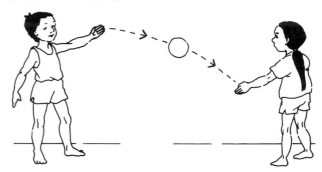

How many times can you pat the ball to each other? Count. See if you can beat your score.

Unit 1: Travelling, sending and receiving, lesson 7 ▷

Theme: travelling and sending egg-shaped balls

Purpose: PoS General b1; d1

Activity bank: Games/athletics: 6, 8, 30

Resources: one rugby ball per pupil

Introduction:
Play 'Stuck in the mud' (see Games/athletics activity 30).

What happens to your breathing when you stop running?

Development:
Work alone: carry an egg-shaped ball around the work area.
Throw and catch the ball yourself.
How many times do you think you will be able to throw and catch the ball without dropping it?
How many times were you successful?
Put down/pick up the ball as you travel around the area with ball tucked under arm.

Which is the easiest?
Roll the ball along a line, run after and retrieve it.

Run with ball under the right/left arm.

Bounce ball on floor and retrieve/catch.
Why is the rugby ball difficult to bounce and catch?
Work in pairs: find a way of sending the ball.
Roll to partner for them to retrieve.
Bounce to partner for them to catch.
Throw to partner for them to catch.
Kick the ball to partner to stop, then kick or throw it back.

Conclusion:
Work in pairs: A at the front, B following behind. A has the ball, both run playing follow-my-leader, when A puts the ball on the floor B picks it up and becomes the leader. Repeat.

Teacher gives command to place the ball down in the beginning, leading to the children making their own decision on when to put it down.

Unit 1: Travelling, sending and receiving, lesson 8 ▷

Theme: throwing and aiming in pairs

Purpose: PoS General b1

Activity bank: Core: 2, 4, 5, 6; Games/athletics 16

Resources: medium balls, hoops

Introduction:
Revise locomotion. Show your teacher what you can do. Introduce hopscotch.
In pairs, play follow-my-leader. Partner A at front links together different locomotor skills, e.g. hopping followed by skipping followed by jumping. B follows. Swap over and repeat.
Encourage: change pathway, change direction, change speed.

Development:
Work in pairs using a medium ball. A stands behind line, B stands behind A. B rolls ball away from the line, partner runs to receive it, then runs back.

Swap over and repeat.
Repeat above, but bounce the ball away from the line. Swap over.
Partners face each other four metres apart. One rolls ball for partner to walk towards to receive. Swap over.

Repeat for bouncing.
Increase the speed of the bounce/roll, encouraging partner to run towards the ball.
How fast can you roll the ball?

Conclusion:
Work in pairs using two hoops, one close by, the other further away. Aim to bounce the ball into each hoop.
Partner stands opposite to retrieve the ball bounced by the other.
Aim to bounce the ball into the hoop stipulated by partner.

Make up a game that involves bouncing the ball and aiming it into the hoops.
Think of the rules and how to score a point. Play the game. Demonstrate your game to another group.

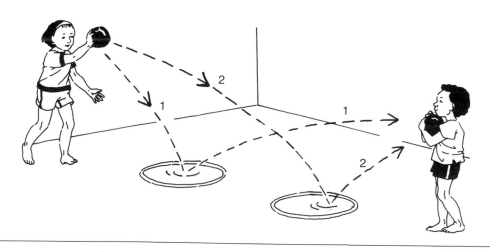

100

Unit 1: Travelling, sending and receiving, lesson 9 ▷

Theme: send and receiving activities in small groups

Purpose: PoS General b1; b2

Activity bank: Games/athletics: 8, 24, 25, 26, 27, 31

Resources: variety of balls, hoops, grids

Introduction:
Play the 'Statues game' (see Games/athletics activity 31).
In pairs, one stands still, partner runs in and out of the statues.
On command, stop and go back to partner. Swap over and repeat.

Development:
In pairs, choose a ball.
Move towards partner using hands or feet.
Send the ball to partner.
Combine the skills of travelling and sending.

Use both hands and feet. Try one then the other.
Which are you most successful at?
Select a different type of ball.
Try sending using hands then feet.
Which method of sending propels the ball the furthest?

Conclusion:
In pairs: 1 + 1 (co-operation).
Work in a grid with a hoop at the end for the 'team' to score into.

Pass the ball at least twice before bouncing the ball into the hoop.

In fours: three working with one observing, 2 v 1.
Work in grid with hoop as goal (as above).
The team of two aim to pass the ball to partner and to bounce the ball in the nearest hoop, in order to score a goal. The defender cannot touch the other two players. After three goals, swap over. Each person should take a turn at being the defender, the observer.

Unit 2: Development of using games equipment, lesson 1 ▷

Theme: using a bat

Purpose: PoS General a1, a5; b1

Activity bank: Core: 3; Games/athletics: 7, 21, 32

Resources: small balls, medium balls, bats

Introduction:
In pairs, play 'Tag' games (see Games/athletics activity 32).

How long does it take you to tag your partner?

Development:
Work alone: pat ball in air using right/left hand.
Pat ball on the floor using right/left hand.
Introduce the bat.
Find ways of travelling around the space with a bat and ball.
Develop an 'egg and spoon' activity, i.e. balance the ball on the bat or use a series of taps.

Travel around the space rolling the ball with bat.

Make shapes on the floor, e.g. square, circle, triangle.

Walk/run around obstacles balancing/tapping the ball on the bat.

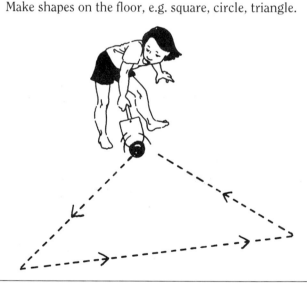

Conclusion:
Working on your own, keep the ball in the air using the bat as many times as you can.
How many times did you hit the ball?
Hitting the ball on the floor with the bat, can you write your name on the floor?
How high can you hit the ball in the air using the bat?
Make sure that it comes back to the ground close to you.

Unit 2: Development of using games equipment, lesson 2 ▷

Theme: developing hitting skills

Purpose: PoS General a1; b2

Activity bank: Core: 2, 3; Games/athletics 7, 21

Resources: small balls, medium balls, bats

Introduction:
Work in pairs: A is the statue, B has the bat and ball.
Using the bat, B chooses how to travel with the ball.

B takes the ball around the statues for thirty seconds.
Swap over. Repeat.

Development:
Use right/left hand to hit the ball against a wall.

Which is your favourite hand?
How many times are you successful with each hand?
Repeat using your favoured hand.
Hit the ball using the bat against the wall.
How many times were you successful?
Try hitting the ball up high against the wall.
Try hitting the ball low against the wall.
Which was the easiest?

How many times can you hit the ball without letting it
out of your control?
Repeat using a bat.

Conclusion:
Work in pairs: one with bat, the other with ball. Throw
ball to partner, can they hit it back to you? Can you
catch it?

Try this three times. Repeat, changing roles. How many
times did you catch it?
Repeat, trying to beat your first score.
Progression: return to partner's right side and left side.
Return to partner, high and low.
Send to partner's bat on the left side and the right side.
How can you make it difficult for your partner?

103

Unit 2: Development of using games equipment, lesson 3 ▷

Theme: developing hitting in pairs (basic net games)

Purpose: PoS General b2

Activity bank: Games/athletics 7, 21, 24, 26, 27

Resources: small balls, medium balls, bats, obstacles (bean bags, quoits, markers etc.)

Introduction:
Move around the obstacles set out, patting and catching the ball yourself.

Change pathway.
Pat the ball on the floor whilst moving around the obstacles.

Development:
Work in pairs: use a medium/small ball depending on ability level.
Throw and catch ball with partner.
Introduce two markers to throw between, partner stands on the other side to catch and return.
Use the line made by markers.
One partner hits ball with hand and bounces it for other partner to catch. Repeat.
Try the above using a bat.

Conclusion:
Choose whether to use your hand or a bat (depending on level of ability).

Play a 1 + 1 game (co-operate with partner). Make up your own rules.
How many consecutive touches did you get?

Unit 2: Development of using games equipment, lesson 4 ▷

Theme: basic hockey

Purpose: PoS General a5

Activity bank: Games/athletics: 2, 33, 37b

Resources: small balls, medium balls, hockey sticks, coloured bands

Introduction:
Play the 'Cat and mouse' game (see Games/athletics activity 33).
Work in pairs. Each player tucks a band into the back of their shorts or skirt.
Facing their partner, without contact, each player tries to grab the band from their opponent.
Score a point for every successful attempt.

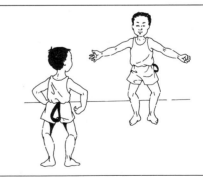

Development:
Work alone: using a stick and a medium/small ball each, take the ball around the space.
Stop and start on command.
Choose when to stop and start.

Change pathway.
Change direction.
Move in and out of obstacles.
How many obstacles can you travel around in thirty seconds?

Conclusion:
Work in pairs: one person at the front, the other behind them.
Shadow partner, dribbling the ball around the area.
On command, A controls the ball and gives it to B. Swap

over and repeat.
To progress, the person at the front attempts to lose the follower.
Watch out for the rest of the group.

Unit 2: Development of using games equipment, lesson 5 ▷

Theme: sending and receiving using hockey sticks

Purpose: PoS General b1

Activity bank: Games/Athletics 2, 37b

Resources: medium balls, small balls, hockey sticks, obstacles (bean bags, quoits, markers etc.)

Introduction:
Travel around the obstacles with the stick and ball.
Change speed on command.
Pupils choose when to change speed.

As you are travelling around the area, on command, follow somebody close by you. Follow them until the next command.
Repeat, choosing somebody different.

Development:
On your own, using a hockey stick, send the ball against a wall, then retrieve.

In pairs: use two markers to make a 'gate'. One person stands on either side of the gate. Push ball to partner, they control and return.

How many times do you think you can get the ball through the gate?
In one minute how many times can you get it through the gate?

Conclusion:
In pairs: use two markers to make a 'gate'. Try to hit the ball past your partner and through the gate.
How do you think you can get the ball past your partner?

How many points did you score?
Swap over each time.

Unit 2: Development of using games equipment, lesson 6 ▷

Theme: sending and receiving in pairs using hockey sticks

Purpose: PoS General b2

Activity bank: Games/athletics 2

Resources: small balls, hockey sticks, markers

Introduction:
Work in pairs: label each person A or B.
Both travel around the whole area with a small ball using a hockey stick.
On command, A stops, controlling their ball, whilst B travels towards them with their ball. B has to plan the quickest route to A.
When all the class are in pairs and stationary, repeat, changing roles.

Development:
Work in pairs: face each other.
A sends ball to B's right, B returns to A's right. Repeat three/four times.
A sends ball to B's left, B returns to A's left. Repeat three/four times.
B stands in front of A.
A sends ball into space, B runs after it and retrieves.
A then runs to catch B.
When they are together, B then sends the ball into a space and A retrieves it.
Repeat a number of times.

Conclusion:
Work in pairs. Set up a simple skill circuit, as shown.
Player A pushes the ball through the gate, chases after it, controls it then travels back to the start with the ball.

A passes the ball to B, who repeats the circuit.
How many times can you complete the circuit in a minute?

Unit 2: Development of using games equipment, lesson 7 ▷

Theme: individualising basic games skills; making games in pairs

Purpose: PoS General a2; b2

Activity bank: Games/athletics 2, 4, 6, 7, 8, 9, 21, 22, 25, 26, 27, 28, 29

Resources: variety of balls, sticks, bats, cones, hoops

Introduction: Choose your own equipment, i.e. a ball and/or an implement.	Travel around the area with the equipment. Stop/start. Take the ball on a journey around the space.
Development: With a partner, decide which equipment you will use. Practise travelling with the equipment.	Moving into a space, find many different ways of sending and receiving the ball.
Conclusion: Make up a game with the equipment chosen. This game should be in co-operation with your partner, i.e. 1 + 1. Using a target, e.g. a cone or a hoop, find a way of	scoring a 'goal'. Make up another game. This game should be in competition with your partner, i.e. 1 v 1. Demonstrate your games to another pair.

Unit 2: Development of using games equipment, lesson 8 ▷

Theme: developing games making – part 1

Purpose: PoS General a2; b2

Activity bank: Games/athletics 10, 34

Resources: foam balls; variety of balls, bats, sticks, obstacles (bean bags, quoits, markers etc.)

Introduction: Play 'dodgeball' (see Games/athletics activity 34). Work in a group of 4/5. One person stands in the middle with the others forming a circle round them. Roll a foam ball, aim to hit the middle person on the ankles.	After thirty seconds, change the middle person. Find a way of outwitting the person in the middle. Is this game getting you puffing?
Development: In pairs: make up your own obstacle course. Use equipment of your choice. Shadow your partner around the obstacles using the equipment.	Now work alongside your partner, taking them around the obstacle course and sharing the ball by sending it to each other.
Conclusion: In co-operation with your partner make up a simple game (1 + 1) using your chosen equipment. Teacher explains in simple terms the meaning of a rule.	Pupils make up one rule to help their game. Pick out certain pairs to tell the rest of the class the rule that they have made up.

Unit 2: Development of using games equipment, lesson 9 ▷

Theme: Developing games making – part 2

Purpose: PoS General a2; b2; c1

Activity bank: Games/athletics: see whole bank

Resources: foam balls; variety of balls; variety of implements; markers, cones, hoops, bean bags/quoits to mark out the grids

Introduction:
Working in small groups, play 'dodgeball', as in lesson 8.

Development:
Work in pairs, using a ball, implement and target (e.g. cone or hoop).
Find a space for you and your partner to work in. Mark it out using the markers available.

Make up and play your game (1 + 1) helping each other. In your game decide how you will travel with the ball using the implement.
Decide how you will score a 'goal'.

Conclusion:
Show your game to another pair.
They describe how you play your game and how you score a point.

Swap over. You describe the other pair's game.

Unit 3: Introduction to the games structure, lesson 1 ▷

Theme: individual game with large ball using hands

Purpose: PoS General a2, a5; b1; d1

Activity bank: Core: 2, 3; Games/athletics: 8, 24, 26, 27

Resources: large balls; target on the wall/basket on the floor; hoops

Introduction:
Running activities concentrating on speed.
On your own run from one line to another and back, as fast as you can.
How many times can you run there and back in thirty seconds?

Development:
On your own, throw and catch a large ball.
Throw it in the air, bounce it on the floor, throw it against a wall.
Using a target on the wall or a hoop/basket on the floor, throw the ball against/into the target.
How many times can you hit the target?

Conclusion:
On your own using the large ball and a hoop, make up and play a game.
How do you score a goal/point?

Show your game to a partner.
They try to play your game.
Swap over.

Unit 3: Introduction to the games structure, lesson 2 ▷

Theme: individual game with large ball using feet

Purpose: PoS General a2; b2; d1

Activity bank: Core: 3; Games/athletics: 4, 5, 35

Resources: large balls, markers, cones

Introduction:
Running activities for distance.

Take a 'journey'. Teacher makes up a story (see Games/athletics activity 35 for an example).

Development:
On your own with a large ball, find ways of travelling using the feet.
Use one or two cones as a target. Send the ball at/through the target. Chase after the ball to retrieve.
How many times did you hit the target or get the ball through the target?
Start 10 metres away from the cone(s), travel to the target, when you are close by, send the ball, attempting to hit the cone or get the ball through the cones.

Conclusion:
On your own, use a large ball and feet.
Make up a game using two cones.
How do you score a point/goal?

Show your game to a partner.
They copy your game.
Swap over.

Unit 3: Introduction to the games structure, lesson 3 ▷

Theme: partner games with large ball using hands

Purpose: PoS General a2; b2; d1

Activity bank: Core: 4; Games/athletics: 8, 10, 22, 24, 26, 27, 28

Resources: chalked lines, bean bags, large balls, hoops, cones

Introduction:
On your own, jump from two feet to two feet.
Find a space to jump into, have a rest, then jump into another space.
Find a line to stand behind. (Have a bean bag in your hand ready to use as a marker.)
Jump from behind the line as far as you can.
Put the bean bag on the spot where your heels landed.
Measure the jump with your feet.
Repeat two/three times. Try to beat your distance each time.

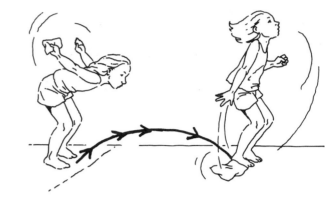

Development:
In pairs: using hands and a large ball, travel to partner and find a suitable way of passing the ball to them.
Travel with ball around your partner, then send it to them when you are close to them.
Facing your partner, send the ball to their right side, then left side.

Conclusion:
In pairs: using hands and a large ball, co-operate together to make up a game, i.e. 1 + 1.
Use a cone or hoop as a target to shoot at or into.
How do you score a goal/point?
Show the class examples of the games made up.

Unit 3: Introduction to the games structure, lesson 4 ▷

Theme: partner games with large ball using feet

Purpose: PoS General a2; b2; c1; d1

Activity bank: Core: 4; Games/athletics: 4, 5, 23, 25, 37a

Resources: chalked lines, bean bags, large balls, obstacles (bean bags, cones, markers etc.), targets (cones, hoops, baskets etc.)

Introduction:
On your own, practise jumping from two feet to two feet in a space, concentrating on distance.
In pairs: start behind a line, A jumps and makes a mark with a bean bag. Measure jump with feet (as in lesson 3).
B then starts behind the line and repeats, attempting to beat their partner.
Repeat a number of times.
Who jumped further?
(Ensure that children of similar height are paired together for this as their leg length determines the distance that they jump.)

Development:
Work in pairs, using feet and a large ball. Place obstacles in the area. Travel in and out of the markers randomly, passing the ball to each other with the feet.
Practise sending and receiving the ball with the feet from the right and the left.
Which send does your partner find it easiest to receive the ball from?

Conclusion:
Work in pairs, using feet and a large ball.
Play a co-operative game, i.e. 1 + 1.
Choose a target, e.g. a cone, to shoot at.
How do you score a goal/point?
Teacher gives a simple explanation of the meaning of a rule and asks the children to think of one rule for their game.
Listen to examples of rules from the rest of the class.

Unit 3: Introduction to the games structure, lesson 5 ▷

Theme: introduction to a 'net game'

Purpose: PoS General a2; b2; c1; d1

Activity bank: Core: 4; Games/athletics: 21, 29

Resources: space on a wall to make a mark for height, small balls, medium balls, markers, bats

Introduction:
Practise jumping for height individually.
Stand still, take off from two feet, jump as high as you can.
Stand sideways on close to wall, reach up as high as you can without jumping or standing on tip-toes.
Make a mark on the wall, then try to jump past that mark.

Development:
Work in pairs: A has the bat, B has the ball.
B sends the ball for A to return with the bat, B catches the ball. Try three attempts, then swap over.

Progress to both players having a bat. If pairs have difficulties, then allow them to send and return the ball using their hand. They decide whether to use their hand or a bat.

Conclusion:
In pairs, play a competitive game, i.e. 1 v 1.
Place three markers at an equal distance between the two players to form the 'net'.
Play a simple 'net' game where the aim is to get the ball over the 'net' and past your partner.

Score one point for every successful attempt.
Who is first to score three points?
How can you beat your partner, i.e. how can you get the ball past them?

Unit 3: Introduction to the games structure, lesson 6 ▷

Theme: introduction to an 'invasion game' using hockey sticks

Purpose: PoS General a2; c1; d1

Activity bank: Core: 4; Games/athletics 2, 37b

Resources: hockey sticks, small/medium balls, obstacles (bean bags, cones, markers etc.)

Introduction:
As in lesson 5, jumping, concentrating on height.
With a partner of similar height: each make a mark on the wall when stretched up high without standing on tiptoes or jumping.
Try to beat your partner's mark by jumping up high above it.
Who could jump the highest?

Development:
In pairs, travel, send and receive using hockey sticks and a medium/small ball.
(The size of the ball will be dependent on the level of skill of the players.)
Use obstacles and 'gates'. Partners stand on either side of the markers and aim the ball between them.
How many times did you get the ball through the 'gate'?

Conclusion:
In pairs, partners face each other with their respective cone (goal) behind them.
Start with sticks together with the ball 'sandwiched' between them. Take it in turns to say 'Go'.

On command, each player attempts to get the ball to their opponent's cone.
If they pass their opponent's cone they score one point.
Repeat. How can you outwit your partner and get to their cone before they get to yours?

Unit 3: Introduction to the games structure, lesson 7 ▷

Theme: small group games; keeping possession; using hands

Purpose: PoS General a2; b2; c1; d1

Activity bank: Core: 4, 5, 6; Games/athletics: 8, 24, 26, 27

Resources: large/medium balls (size of the ball will depend on the child's level of skill)

Introduction:
On your own, practise hopping (one foot to the same foot), stepping (one foot to the other foot) and jumping (two feet to two feet) as isolated skills.
Then try to link them together, e.g. hop then jump, jump then step.

Development:
In pairs, pass the large/medium ball by throwing and by bouncing.
Do this when stationary, then when moving into a space.
How can you let your partner know that you are ready to catch the ball?
Encourage your partner to run into a space, signalling with the hand, to catch the ball.

Conclusion:
Work in groups of four in a space, 3 v 1. Can the team of three keep the ball in their possession for ten seconds?

NB: Pupils are not allowed to travel with the ball.
Allow them to move in any area they choose as long as they do not make contact with other members of the class.
The team of three think of different ways of keeping the ball from the other person.
For progression, restrict their movement to within a suitably marked out grid.
Swap over constantly, to ensure that all players have a turn in each role.
When you are in the team of three, count how many times the ball was kept in your possession.
When you are alone count how many times you intercepted the ball from the other team.

Unit 3: Introduction to the games structure, lesson 8 ▷

Theme: small group games; keeping possession and scoring a goal

Purpose: PoS General a1, a2; c1; d1

Activity bank: Core: 4, 5, 6; Games/athletics: see whole bank

Resources: variety of balls, hoops, cones, markers, grids

Introduction:
Hopping, stepping and jumping in isolation.
Combination jumps: practise putting two jumps together, e.g. hop then step, jump then step, step then hop etc. Choose a combination of your jumps.

Development:
In pairs, choose a ball and choose use of hands or feet.
Practise travelling, sending and receiving the ball, using activities from previous lessons.

Conclusion:
Work in groups of four.
Together choose a ball, then decide on the body part you are going to use to travel and to send and receive the ball with.
Work within a suitably sized grid.
Decide on a 'rule' for how to score a point/goal.
Highlight any good examples in the class.

Unit 3: Introduction to the games structure, lesson 9 ▷

Theme: development of passing within a team; scoring a goal

Purpose: PoS General a2; b2; c1; d1

Activity bank: Core: 4, 5, 6

Resources: variety of balls, grids, bean bags/markers

Introduction:
As in last lesson, combine two jumps, e.g. hop then step etc.
Choose your favourite combination jump, then challenge a partner to a 'jump off'.
Stand behind a line with a bean bag/marker and place it where the heels are after the combination jump. Partner tries to beat the distance by using the same combination jump, or by using their own combination jump.
Which was the most successful?
Who could jump the further?

Development:
In pairs, choose a ball.
Practise moving in and out of spaces in order to catch the ball from partner.
Choose a space to move into.
Then move to using a grid, stay within the boundaries.

Conclusion:
Work in fours, 2 v 2.
Use hands and a large ball.
Work in a grid.
Aim to bounce the ball over the end line in order to score a point/goal.
Start on the opposite line.
Each team decides on the easiest way of getting the ball to the other end and over the line.
At first, travelling with the ball is allowed, however with greater skill level, passing and receiving only is allowed.
Pick out good examples from the class.

OUTDOOR AND ADVENTUROUS ACTIVITIES

ABOUT OUTDOOR AND ADVENTUROUS ACTIVITIES ▶

Outdoor and Adventurous Activities extend through all key stages of the National Curriculum as one of the six areas of the foundation subject of PE. The frequently held belief that outdoor education is mainly concerned with outdoor pursuit activities such as rock climbing, white water canoeing, caving and strenuous mountain walks has meant that many teachers, particularly in the primary sector, have been reluctant to become involved. However, we now have to consider Outdoor Activities for all age ranges and outdoor education must be considered as a cross-curricular medium at all levels.

With a little imagination, the scope for a stimulating and creative area of learning is limitless. Throughout the key stages Outdoor and Adventurous Activities encourage the learning of skills and knowledge to explore and investigate the potential for physical activities in our rich and varied environment, with safety and enjoyment. Understanding and recognising opportunities for physical activity in the immediate and distant environment are essential if we are to provide a rounded physical education experience. By the time pupils finish their school education, it is also essential that they appreciate the frailty of our environment and are aware that an individual can play a role in helping to preserve it for future generations, yet continue to use it for healthy and challenging physical activity. Outdoor and Adventurous Activities should enable pupils to develop this not alone, but in a cross-curricular context, as part of their whole education.

NATIONAL CURRICULUM REQUIREMENTS AT KEY STAGE 1 ▶

All statements from the programme of study (general) are relevant to outdoor and adventurous activities. You will find these developed in the units of work that follow.

Pupils should:

a1 be given opportunities to develop a wide range of simple movements in a variety of activities with and without equipment.

a2 be encouraged to recognise and make up simple rules, and work within them.

a3 be guided and encouraged to use movement to show moods and feelings and respond to simple rhythms and contrasting stimuli.

a4 be taught to link movements with increasing control to show changes of direction or levels and variations of speed, tension or rhythm.

a5 be helped to recognise and follow safety procedures, including lifting, carrying and moving equipment.

b1 be encouraged to practise and perform simple skills.

b2 be encouraged to improve performance as they work alone, and when ready, in co-operation with a partner.

c1 be given the opportunity to describe what they and others have done in physical education, and how they did it, using simple, functional and aesthetic terms.

d1 be made aware of the changes that happen to their bodies during exercise.

The programme of study (activity specific) for this area of PE is as follows:

> Pupils should:
>
> • explore the potential for physical activities within the immediate environment.
> (This encourages teachers to use the whole school environment and to examine what opportunities may exist in less familiar terrain).
> • undertake simple orientation activities.
> (This is taught in Year 2, Unit 2, concentrating on the relatively difficult concept of plan).

> • apply physical skills out of doors on suitable equipment.
> (This is concerned with using apparatus that is usually a permanent outdoor fixture, but may include portable equipment).
> • develop an awareness of basic safety practices.
> (This includes safe practice inside and out as well as the more recognised codes of behaviour essential for the safety of pupils in and outside the school environment).

Note: the wording in brackets has been added by the authors.

TEACHING OUTDOOR AND ADVENTUROUS ACTIVITIES AT KEY STAGE 1

For Outdoor and Adventurous Activities 18 lesson plans (divided into two units) are provided for Reception/Year 1 and the same for Year 2. Despite the title 'Outdoor Activities', many of these lessons can be taken either inside or out. This will not only be determined by the weather and confidence of the teacher, but also by the facilities available to the school.

Although the lessons here are of relatively short duration and are specific to Outdoor and Adventurous Activities, there is much overlap with other areas of PE particularly in the early units. The teacher is also encouraged to combine with other subject areas to make more use of any time available, to maximise potential for exploring the immediate environment.

Within Key Stage 1, there are four programmes of study (activity specific) as set out in the National Curriculum requirements. You will not find that individual units of work cover particular statements, apart from Year 2, Unit 2 which is specifically concerned with simple orientation tasks.

The lesson plans are supported by two activity banks. The Core Movement Skills Activity Bank provides specific material related to the core movements of walking, stopping and running. The Outdoor and Adventurous Activity Bank provides additional material that will enable you as the teacher to develop the lessons further. Variations to specific games and activities are given, along with how some of these may be developed when appropriate.

The model lessons

Two model lessons are provided to illustrate planning and evaluating issues. These kinds of considerations need to be built into all your work in this area of PE.

Model Lesson 1

In this lesson, the teacher should ensure all explanations are clear to the whole group by using imaginative storylines, to create enthusiasm, particularly at the start of the lesson. Pupils should be fully aware that they must move to an 'island' when the teacher says 'Stop'. As the lesson progresses the teacher should allow more time after the command 'Stop' for the pupils to achieve a position on their island. Pupils should be encouraged to help each other to achieve this objective and should be grouped according to size and ability to co-operate with others, to try and ensure a mixed ability range for each island. This will hopefully allow the less co-operative to become more involved. By discussing their performance and watching a particularly successful group on the activity, all pupils should recognise how they can help each other. The teacher should always be alert to any safety issues that may arise, e.g. pupils pushing on the mats or hoops, running into each other, etc.

Model Lesson 2

Prior to the lesson the teacher should lay out the rope or string trail, covering as varied a terrain as possible. The rope should be kept at ground level and never above a pupil's waist. The teacher's demonstration should emphasize the need to keep to the trail, yet looking for objects to both sides of the rope. Pupils should begin the trail with an interval between each pair, with a larger interval when the trail follows a more adventurous route to prevent any backlog or collisions. Any objects placed by the teacher should be close enough to the trail so pupils are not tempted to leave it and search randomly. It will be necessary for the teacher to concentrate attention particularly on areas where the trail passes over or through apparatus to ensure safety. Early in the lesson it should be possible to include some cross-curricular comments with regard to the collection of hard and soft objects such as twigs, leaves and stones. By the end of the lesson the pupils should be able to follow a rope trail over a variety of terrain.

Model lesson 1: Reception/Year 1, unit 2, lesson 9 ▷

Theme: adventure activities; small group work

Purpose: PoS General a1, a2, a4, a5; b2

Activity bank: Core: 1

Resources: mats, hoops and chalk shapes

Activity	Organisation		Teaching points	
Introduction: Teacher explains each piece of apparatus is an 'island' (surrounded by water).	Mats, hoops, chalk marks/circles, arranged around hall. Split children up and have a group on each piece of apparatus ('island').		Explain that children must stay within apparatus.	
Development: Teacher explains: On 'Go' move to another 'island'. On 'Stop' (or whistle) all children to be on an 'island'. Practice run.	Children to listen and practice.	(P)	Teacher asks: 'Can you fit everyone on the 'island'?'	(EV)
Teacher asks pupils to sit, then stand, then lie down.	Children to sit, stand, lie down.	(P)	What takes up more space (sitting, lying, standing)?	(EV)
On 'Go' children move to another 'island'. On 'Stop' all children to be on 'islands' – sitting. Repeat.	Children to practice moving to other 'islands'	(P)		
Conclusion: Teacher explains 'islands' are going to be smaller (or reduced in number).	'Islands' to be reduced enough to fit all children standing close together. Children to listen and watch teacher.			
Children to practice trying to fit on different 'islands' sitting.	Children to practice. Children to try and fit everyone on the 'islands' sitting.	(P) (PL)	Can everyone fit on the 'islands' sitting? Can everyone fit on the 'islands' lying? Can everyone fit on the 'islands' standing?	(EV) (EV)

Model lesson 2: Year 2, unit 1, lesson 3 ▷

Theme: exploring school environment

Purpose: PoS General a1, a2, a4; b2, c1

Activity bank: Core: 1, 2

Resources: school grounds; rope trail; leaves, twigs, pebbles

Activity	Organisation	Teaching points	
Introduction: Recap previous lesson.	All children sitting together.	What did you collect last lesson? Where did it come from? Recap on hard/soft objects.	(EV)
Show children rope trail and explain.	All children go to rope trail which is on flat ground. Teacher to demonstrate following rope.		

117

...omething soft/hard. (PL)	In pairs, follow trail. Teacher also moves around trail keeping group together, walking. (P)	What did you find? Was it soft/hard? (EV) How many different things did we find? (EV)
Show children second rope trail and explain.	Trail to follow more adventurous course through apparatus, up and down steps, under mats, etc.	
Collect three different items.	In pairs, follow trail. Teacher checks movement over apparatus. (!)	What did you find on this trail? (EV) Was this trail more difficult? (EV)

Conclusion:

Repeat, collecting more items on same trail. (PL)	Teacher may place items strategically to provide greater challenge. In pairs, follow trail. (P) Teacher checks movement over apparatus. (!)	
Children to show what they have found. (P)	Ensure all children have the opportunity to show what they collected.	What did you find? (EV)

OUTDOOR AND ADVENTUROUS ACTIVITY BANK

Activity 1: Animals and their dens
The children move around yard or grass area, making appropriate noises, but when the hunter (teacher or later a child suitably dressed) appears they try to hide in dens and be silent. When he has gone away they come out again. Dens could be drawn on playground or hoops used on grass. As the game progresses the hunter can catch the slower animals.

Activity 2: Suspension bridge
In groups of five to eight, children make a chain to stretch as far across an area as possible. They should be linked together and not lying down.

Activity 3: Ordering on a bench or log
Six to eight children stand on a bench. Ask them to order themselves by height. If successful, ask them to order themselves without stepping off the bench. Further development may be to ask them to order themselves alphabetically or chronologically. To make it more difficult, you could introduce limited instructions (e.g. one child only to speak) or even total silence.

Activity 4: Tying and untying knots
In small groups of two to four, tie as many knots as possible in a skipping rope (or similar), in one to four minutes. The tied rope is then passed on to another group, who have to untie the knots. This can be a straight race or against the clock. Further development may be introducing blindfolds. This exercise should encourage working with partners or in small groups and manual dexterity in handling ropes.

Activity 5: Hide and seek
Variations on this simple game can be introduced with imaginative story lines, e.g. shepherd and lost sheep, mountain search and rescue.

Activity 6: From A to B
Numerous challenges can be designed to present initially a type of obstacle course, progressing to using apparatus in a 'problem solving' manner, to enable an individual or small group to achieve an objective. This activity will be greatly determined by the school environment and equipment available. This may include fixed apparatus such as climbing frames, tunnels, swings etc, as well as standard gymnastic and games apparatus. In addition to this the following items are examples of equipment that can be used to creative effect: tyres, barrels, inflated inner tubes, ropes, blankets, poles, logs and planks.

At this stage further environmental exploration and orientation exercises will be limited by the child's conceptual development in other areas of the curriculum.

LESSON PLANS FOR RECEPTION/YEAR 1

Unit 1, lesson 1

Theme: personal movement

Purpose: PoS General a1; b1

Activity bank: Core: 1, 2, 3

Resources: none

Introduction:
Walk around work area. Use of commands (Stop/Go).

Pupils should aim for no contact and use of personal space.

Development:
Repeat introduction with these variations:
1 walk toward objects (e.g. window, teacher, door, gate, fence etc).

2 walk with head held high and stiff back.
3 walk, stop, sit down. Repeat.
Vary command signals to start and stop (e.g. whistle, voice, clap).

Conclusion:
Follow the leader. Either the whole class follows teacher or divide into small groups with a pupil leader for each group.

Follow route around, to include walking, sitting and possibly running.

Unit 1, lesson 2

Theme: personal movement

Purpose: PoS General a1; b1

Activity bank: Core: 1, 2

Resources: string, chalk or markers

Introduction:
Walk, stop, walk, stop, sit down.
Try to encourage a sense of spatial awareness, no contact.

Vary commands (clap, voice, whistle).

Development:
Repeat introduction but:
1 use varied walks: swinging arms, stiff legs, long strides, stamping

2 use running: fast/slow, small/big steps, noisy/quiet
3 follow a prescribed route: marked out with string, chalk lines or markers.

Conclusion:
Follow prescribed route running.

119

Unit 1, lesson 3

Theme: personal movement

Purpose: PoS General a1, a2, a4; b2

Activity bank: Core: 2, 3

Resources: hoops, music

Introduction:
Reinforce running/stopping, walking/stopping from last lesson.

Walk/run into hoops and stop.

Development:
Play 'Musical Hoops'. When music stops, run to the nearest hoop.

To start, ensure sufficient hoops for two children per hoop.
Repeat and reduce hoops progressively.

Conclusion:
On command, run around area linking jumping into hoops and stopping.

Teacher creates a story: for example pupils chased by wild animal and to escape they can hide in the hoops.
Children put hoops away.

Unit 1, lesson 4

Theme: movement over apparatus

Purpose: PoS General a1, a4, a5; b1, b2

Activity bank: Core: 1, 2, 3, 4

Resources: hoops, mats

Introduction:
Teacher demonstrates jumping, first a single foot jump

(left to right and vice versa), then jumping using both feet. Pupils practice.

Development:
Run around using various jumps on to mats, into hoops etc.
Link hoops and mats to form several circuits (up to ten objects in any one circuit). Use various jumps. The area outside of hoops/mats is a 'crocodile swamp'.

Swamp area
Mat ~ Hoop

Conclusion:
Link the circuits above to form one large circuit.
Pupils to follow teacher or more able child around route.

Children return equipment.

Unit 1, lesson 5

Theme: movement over apparatus

Purpose: PoS General a1, a4, a5; b1, b2

Activity bank: Core: 1, 4

Resources: benches, mats and hoops

Introduction:
Reinforce previous lesson. Practice various jumps onto mats.

Introduce benches: step on to/step off.
Children move benches. Care with carrying and lifting.

Development:
Step on to benches, walk along, step off.
Link benches with mats. Pupils to walk, stepping from benches to mats in a circuit. 'Crocodile swamp' is the floor.
Jump on to, off and over benches on to mats, following circuit.
Link benches, mats and hoops. Follow circuits.

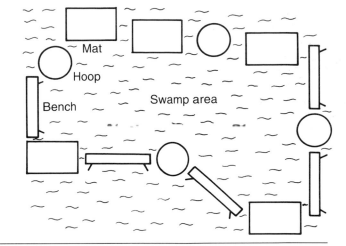

Mat

Hoop

Bench

Swamp area

Conclusion:
Move around on benches and mats with partner, holding hands.

Children return equipment.

Unit 1, lesson 6

Theme: movement over apparatus

Purpose: PoS General a1, a4, a5; b1, b2

Activity bank: Core: 1, 2, 4

Resources: benches, mats, hoops and bean bags

Introduction:
Some children assist with layout of equipment.
Repeat circuits of benches, mats and hoops from last lesson.

Try crawling like a dog, sliding like a snake, over mats, under mats.
Be silent.

Development:
As above, carrying 'parcel' (bean bag) to deliver to 'post box'.

As above, collecting several bean bags on route. Bean bags placed at different collection points. Repeat, delivering several bean bags on route.

Conclusion:
Pupils to work with partner carrying a larger 'parcel' to deliver to 'post box'. This may be a football or similar

sized object.
Repeat, collecting different object.
Return equipment.

Unit 1, lesson 7

Theme: movement over apparatus

Purpose: PoS General a1, a2, a4, a5; b1

Activity bank: Core: 1, 2

Resources: benches, mats, hoops, climbing frame

Introduction:
Stress safety rules on climbing frame (do not climb above head height or third rung; ensure three points of contact at all times; climb down rather than jump, and any other rules applicable to your situation).
Pupils to climb or weave through frame at ground level. Climb to first, second, third rung as applicable. Descend after each level is reached.

Development:
Step from level bench on to climbing frame.
Step from bench through frame on to another bench.

Conclusion:
Link benches, hoops and climbing frame to form a trail. Teacher relates a story, e.g. pupils to follow circuit to find hidden treasure, follow trail back home or to where you left your lunch.
Return equipment.

Unit 1, lesson 8

Theme: movement over apparatus

Purpose: PoS General a1, a2, a4, a5; b1, b2, d1

Activity bank: Core: 1, 2, 4

Resources: mats, rope swings, scramble net

Introduction:
Stress safety on: rope swing (grip tight, legs around rope, keep feet off the ground); safety net (take your time, place hands and feet carefully, grip tight).
Teacher to demonstrate.

Development:
Work in groups, half class on scramble net, other half on rope swings.
Work on scramble net, go up and down.
Swing on rope to start and finish at the same point, without touching the ground. Progress to starting and finishing at different points.
Change over activities.

Conclusion:
Continue practice of above. Maybe some pupils could attempt a rope climb.

Unit 1, lesson 9

Theme: movement over apparatus; rope trail

Purpose: PoS General a1, a2, a4, a5; b1

Activity bank: Core: 1, 2

Resources: benches, mats, hoops, climbing frame, scramble net, suspended rope swing.

Introduction:
Reinforce safety regulations for climbing frame, rope swing and scramble net.
Teacher explains rope trail (a length of rope, string or chalked line, laid out by teacher, following a trail over, under, or along apparatus) supported by a story, e.g. chocolate dust leading to a chocolate mine.

Development:
Pupils follow rope trail.
This could be done individually or with partner.

Emphasise that they must keep to the trail, no overtaking. They must return to the beginning if they lose the trail.

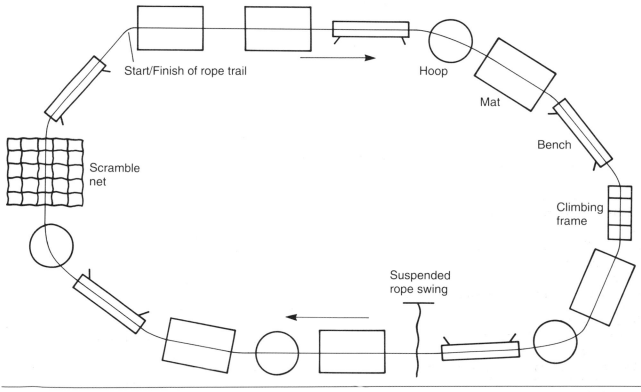

Start/Finish of rope trail

Hoop

Mat

Bench

Scramble net

Climbing frame

Suspended rope swing

Conclusion:
Repeat above, but class is split to start at both ends of the trail, to effect a cross-over.

Return equipment.

Unit 2, lesson 1 ▷

Theme: what to wear

Purpose: PoS General a3, a5; d1

Resources: articles or pictures of clothing

Introduction:
Teacher introduces the subject of clothing. Ask questions like 'Why do we wear clothing?', 'Do we wear the same clothing all year?', 'Do we all wear the same clothing?'

Development:
Pupils work in groups.
Select clothing for summer – hot/dry weather.

Select clothing for winter – cold/wet weather.
Create models or pictures.

Conclusion:
Teacher promotes questions and answers, e.g.
  Who wears lots of clothing? Why?
  Who wears little clothing? Why?

What do you wear to: a) go swimming?
                      b) go to bed?
                      c) go to a party?

Unit 2, lesson 2 ▷

Theme: what to wear

Purpose: PoS General a3, a5; d1

Resources: articles or pictures of clothing

Introduction:
Recap on previous lesson. What would you wear for swimming, games, going to a party?

Development:
Children work in groups. Select clothing for job or activity (e.g. nurse, fireman, cyclist, footballer, games, local walk.)

Create models or pictures.

Conclusion:
Discussion. What can you wear for a local walk later this term?

Selection and review.

Unit 2, lesson 3

Theme: Green Cross Code

Purpose: PoS General a2, a5

Resources: local Road Safety Officer, video and hand-outs

Introduction:
Teacher promotes discussion, questions and answers on road safety.

Development:
Presentation of Green Cross Code.
1 First find a safe place to cross the road and stop.
2 Stand on the pavement near the kerb.
3 Look all around for traffic and listen.
4 If traffic is coming, let it pass, look all around again.
5 When there is no traffic near walk straight across the road.
6 Keep looking and listening for traffic while you cross.

Explanation of Green Cross Code by visiting Road Safety Officer.
Video and hand-outs.

Conclusion:
Recap and discuss.

Unit 2, lesson 4

Theme: Green Cross Code

Purpose: PoS General a2, a5

Resources: Equipment needed to simulate road environment in yard/gym, e.g. cones for traffic lights, chalk lines for road, mats for crossings.

Introduction:
Review previous lesson.
Model road layout, which should include as many situations as possible.

Teacher or pupil demonstrates crossing road.

Development:
Pupils practise crossing road. (Looking left, right etc.)
Repeat.

Practise crossing at pelican crossing.
Discuss. Where do you not cross? (Parked cars, bends etc.)

Conclusion:
Further practice, with as many varied situations as possible.

Unit 2, lesson 5

Theme: Water Safety Code

Purpose: PoS General a2, a5

Resources: LEA Water Safety Officer; video and hand-outs. (Many Local Education Authorities have officers responsible for visiting schools, providing water safety programmes for all levels. Similarly authorities have guidelines on water safety, concentrating at this stage on safe behaviour near water.)

Introduction:
Discuss with pupils where water comes from, where you may find it, why it can be dangerous.

Development:
Explanation of Water Safety Code.

Video and hand-outs.

Conclusion:
Recap. Emphasis on safe behaviour near water.

Unit 2, lesson 6

Theme: adventure games

Purpose: PoS General a1, a3; b1

Activity bank: Core: 1, 3; Outdoor: 1

Resources: hoops/chalk shapes

Introduction:
Pupils run, walk or crawl around and make noises of various animals.

Teacher explains game 'Animals and their dens' (see Outdoor activity 1)

Development:
Play game 'Animals and their dens'.

Teacher reduces number of 'dens' (hoops/chalk circles). 'Hunter' catches unwary/slower animals.

Conclusion:
Make shapes/noises of different animals.

Unit 2, lesson 7

Theme: adventure games	*Activity bank:* Core: 1, 2, 3
Purpose: PoS General a1, a2, a5; b1, b2	*Resources:* hoops and mats

Introduction: In pairs, pupils step through upright hoops, held by partner.	Change over.
Development: As in Introduction, but this time jump through hoops. Change over.	Hoops held in line, separated by mats. Link stepping through hoops with rolling on mats. Change over.
Conclusion: Repeat the second part of the Development section, but	this time holding hands with partner while stepping through hoops.

Unit 2, lesson 8

Theme: adventure games	*Resources:* benches, mats, scarf/towel/cloth to tie ankles
Purpose: PoS General a1, a4; b1, b2	
Activity bank: Core: 1	

Introduction: Walk around holding hands with partner.	Walk around with arm around partner's waist.
Development: Link partners to become 'three-legged'. Walk around without obstacles.	Walk around stepping over, on to and off benches and mats.
Conclusion: Follow course/trail set by teacher.	

Unit 2, lesson 9

Theme: adventure activities/group work	*Activity bank:* Core: 1
Purpose: PoS General a1, a2, a4, a5	*Resources:* mats, hoops and chalk shapes

Introduction: Teacher explains that mats, hoops and chalk shapes represent islands. Groups of three to five to stand on each island.	On command from teacher, pupils move to another island. Repeat.
Development: Pupils should be encouraged to adopt different positions (sitting, standing, lying) on the islands. Progressively either reduce the number of islands	(withdrawing mats, hoops or circles) and increase the number of children in each group, or reduce the size of the islands (smaller hoops, smaller circles).
Conclusion: Teacher promotes discussion by asking 'How many of	you can stand on one island?', 'Can you help each other?', etc.

127

LESSON PLANS FOR YEAR 2

Unit 1, lesson 1

Theme: exploring school environment

Purpose: PoS General a2, a3, a5; c1

Activity bank: Core: 1, 2, 3

Resources: school grounds

Introduction:
Ensure appropriate behaviour and clothing for walk/run.

Explain safety procedures in school grounds.

Development:
Walk around school grounds investigating and recognising characteristic areas: shade/sun, cold/warm,

wet/dry ground, hard/soft ground, noisy/quiet, clean/dirty.

Conclusion:
From a central point teacher indicates a characteristic

area (as above) and children run to such an area and return. Repeat.

Unit 1, lesson 2

Theme: exploring school environment

Purpose: PoS General a2, a3, a5; c1

Activity bank: Core: 1, 2

Resources: school grounds

Introduction:
Recap previous lesson.

Development:
Walk around school grounds investigating and recognising natural items (e.g. flowers, insects, trees,

grass, bushes, leaves – dead and alive) and man-made items (e.g. apparatus, goal posts, concrete yard, sandpit, litter).

Conclusion:
Return to central point.
Pupils then collect (in pairs) three dead, natural items and return.

Repeat, collecting man-made objects.

Unit 1, lesson 3

Theme: exploring school environment

Purpose: PoS General a1, a2, a4; b2; c1

Activity bank: Core: 1, 2

Resources: school grounds, rope/string trail, hoops

Introduction:
Recap previous lesson.
Teacher marks a trail with string or rope and explains to

pupils to follow this trail, collecting on route something hard (e.g. stone, pebble), something soft (e.g. grass, leaves) and one piece of litter.

Development:
Pupils (in pairs) follow trail, which may travel through

apparatus up/down steps, under goal posts, around trees etc, collecting the three items.

Conclusion:
Teacher promotes discussion with questions, e.g.

'Where does the litter come from?', 'What should we do about litter?'

Unit 1, lesson 4

Theme: exploring school environment	*Activity bank:* Core: 1, 2
Purpose: PoS General a1, a2, a4	*Resources:* school grounds, small boxes/bags

Introduction:
Teacher explains the game 'Scavenger Hunt'. Teacher pretends he/she needs items of the following colours to mix together in a potion to stop him/her from getting older: green, brown, white, grey, yellow (or other appropriate colours). (These might be stones, leaves, grass, litter or objects placed by teacher.)

Development:
Pupils collect items from prescribed area (yard, field or surroundings of fixed apparatus). Return to teacher on completion.

Conclusion:
Discuss and appraise items collected.

Unit 1, lesson 5

Theme: exploring school environment	*Activity bank:* Core: 1
Purpose: PoS General a1, a3, a4; b2; c1	*Resources:* blindfolds

Introduction
Pupils work in pairs. One partner is blindfolded, other partner leads around yard by hand. Change roles.

Development:
As introduction, but experience different surfaces (e.g. sand, grass, concrete, soil) and explain what it feels like. As above, but experience touching different features (e.g. trees, windows, walls) by hand. Change roles.

Conclusion:
Discuss and appraise experience of blindfold.

Unit 1, lesson 6

Theme: exploring school environment

Purpose: PoS General a1, a3; b2; c1

Activity bank: Core: 1, 3

Resources: school grounds

Introduction:
Silent movement: on both yard and grass, walk around making as little noise as possible. Repeat, running.

Development:
Have an 'Animal Hunt', with the teacher as the hunter. Pupils walk around over various surfaces (e.g. gravel, concrete, sand, grass) as silently as possible. Teacher withdraws the noisy animals to the side. Repeat, running.

Conclusion:
Teacher asks questions like 'Which surface was the quietest to move over?', 'Which surface made the most noise?'

Unit 1, lesson 7

Theme: adventure games; small group work

Purpose: PoS General a1, a2, a4; b2; c1

Activity bank: Core: 1, 2, 3

Resources: benches

Introduction:
In groups of 4 to 6, step on to benches side by side. Step off. Repeat, holding hands with a partner. Step off backwards and forwards.

Development:
Repeat above, but change positions before stepping off. Arrange benches in squares, four benches to a square. Make as many squares as necessary to allow four to six pupils to a bench. Pupils move around the square, each holding partner's hand, without stepping to ground. Move clockwise/anti-clockwise.

Conclusion:
Move around square in silence. Teacher asks pupils 'Was it hard or easy?', 'Did you enjoy the lesson?'

Unit 1, lesson 8

Theme: adventure games; small group work

Purpose: PoS General a1, a2, a4, a5

Activity bank: Core: 1, 2

Resources: mats, benches, planks and hoops

Introduction:
Stretching exercises, followed by demonstration of correct lifting and carrying techniques.

Development:
Play a 'Swamp' game. The object of the game is to cross the swamp (marked by chalk lines) in small groups. The number and size of groups will be determined by the apparatus available. Pupils can place apparatus wherever they wish to help them cross. They must return to start if they fall into the swamp.

Apparatus: mats, benches, planks and hoops

Examples of solutions are:

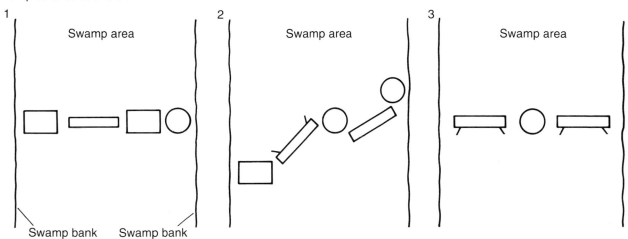

Conclusion:
Teacher asks pupils 'What other apparatus could you use?', Was the activity easy?', 'Did you enjoy the activity?'

Unit 1, lesson 9

Theme: adventure activities; small group work

Purpose: PoS General a2, a4, a5; b1

Activity bank: Core: 1, 2

Resources: mats

Introduction:
Working in groups of four to six lift and carry mat safely, as directed in previous lesson.
Follow a prescribed route.

Development:
Groups travel across 'marsh' using two 'floating' mats only, without touching the 'shark-infested marsh'. Whole group must return to start if one group member falls in.
Observe other groups performing activity.

Conclusion:
Introduce time element.
Discuss the problems encountered.

Unit 2, lesson 1

▷

Theme: orientation (classroom)

Purpose: PoS General b1; c1

Resources: shapes (e.g. triangles, squares, oblongs, circles); paper, pencil, crayons

Introduction:
Place three shapes on paper in simple pattern. Draw around each shape. Remove shapes and look at pattern on paper. This is a plan.

Development:
Replace shapes in original positions.
Remove and replace neighbour's shapes.

Repeat with different shapes.

Conclusion:
Colour outline plans the same colour as the shapes.

Unit 2, lesson 2

▷

Theme: orientation (classroom)

Purpose: PoS General b1; c1

Resources: paper, pencils, rubbers, rulers, small balls; teacher's large plan of classroom

Introduction:
Recap previous lesson.

Position pencil, rubber, ruler, ball on your desk.
Teacher demonstrates plan of desk.

Development:
With partner, draw plan of their desk.
Exchange role with partner.

Teacher guidance essential for initial practice.
Correct and reinforce.

Conclusion:
Teacher shows plan of classroom: emphasis on major features (e.g. door, window, desks, sink)

Children attempt to point to where they sit.

Unit 2, lesson 3

Theme: orientation (classroom)

Purpose: PoS General b1, b2; c1

Resources: paper, pencils, crayons; copies of teacher's outline plan of classroom

Introduction:
Recap last lesson. Emphasis on plan as bird's eye view.
In pairs, pupils mark where they sit on outline plan of classroom.

Provide guidance and help where needed.

Development:
Work with a partner.
Draw on plan the route from the door to your desk, from

your desk to the sink, from the sink to ... etc.
Walk the routes. Reinforce orientation of plan.

Conclusion:
Find object marked on your plan, hidden in the classroom.

These can be marked by the teacher with shapes or symbols on the plan and hidden strategically around the room.

Unit 2, lesson 4

Theme: orientation

Purpose: PoS General b1, b2

Resources: clipboard, crayons, pencils; paper with outline of 'pond'; chalk or rope to mark 'pond' on ground

Introduction:
Teacher explains 'pond' outline on paper. Pupils sit around edge of 'pond' (rope or chalk shape), in pairs.

Either six to ten pupils to each pond or all pupils around a single large pond.

Development:
As teacher places objects (e.g. bean bags, skittles, balls)

in pond, pupils mark each object in correct position on plan. Drawing shapes, symbols or pictures is acceptable.

Conclusion:
Each pupil adds their own object to pond and marks on plan.

Unit 2, lesson 5 ▷

Theme: orientation

Purpose: PoS General a1; b1; c1

Activity bank: Core: 1

Resources: simple plan of hall with easily identifiable objects for each pupil (e.g. bench, climbing frame, mat, chair)

Introduction:
Pupils work in pairs throughout lesson.
Pupils orientate plan and place finger on their position,

e.g. by the door, window or climbing frame. Teacher checks each pair.

Development:
Teacher positions objects around hall corresponding to plan.
Pairs identify shapes, e.g. long/thin rectangle (bench), large square (mat), small square (chair).

Other apparatus can be used, providing it can be easily identified on the plan.
Teacher checks work at each stage.

Conclusion:
Follow trail/line teacher marks on plan around/over objects.

Demonstrations by most able children.

Unit 2, lesson 6 ▷

Theme: orientation

Purpose: PoS General a1; b1, b2; c1

Activity bank: Core: 1

Resources: as previous lesson

Introduction:
Recap and reinforce previous lesson.

Pupils work in pairs throughout lesson.
Find 'treasure' marked on plan (e.g. bean bag, sticker).

Development
In pairs: one child hides 'treasure' and marks position on plan, whilst the other is not looking. Teacher checks position on plan.

Partner to find treasure using plan. No assistance unless required.
Change over.
Observe other class members attempting activity.

Conclusion:
Place additional items around hall and mark on plan.

Unit 2, lesson 7

Theme: orientation

Purpose: PoS General a1; b1, b2; c1

Activity bank: Core: 1

Resources: plan of playground area showing apparatus (by means of a picture, symbol or in plan) for each pair, as shown.

Skittles or cones

Climbing frame

Slide

Hoops

Benches

Mats

Introduction:
Pupils to work in pairs. Walk around playground identifying apparatus on their plans, with guidance. Return to starting point.

Development:
Pupils draw a route/line on their plan and then follow this route, returning to start.

Exchange routes.
Observe other pairs doing activity.

Conclusion:
Review success or failure.

Demonstration by more successful children.

Unit 2, lesson 8

Theme: orientation

Purpose: PoS General a1; b1, b2

Activity bank: Core: 1

Resources: blindfolds; playground grid

Introduction:
Teacher directs children to walk left/right, backwards/forwards.

Stop/go on command.

Development:
Repeat above, but use commands that introduce a number of steps, e.g. follow squares, rectangles, or lines

marked on playground.
Reverse trail.

Conclusion:
Pupils work in pairs. One pupil leads blindfolded partner around trail, as above.

Swap roles.
Teacher promotes discussion on the feelings related to being blindfolded.

Unit 2, lesson 9

Theme: orientation

Purpose: PoS General a2, a5; b2; c1

Activity bank: Core: 1

Resources: simple plan of treasure hunt for each pair. This should be a plan of the area to be used with the

positions of the clues marked. Clues could be lettered cards attached to posts, trees or buildings. Rope or string trail to follow prescribed route.

Introduction:
Teacher explains features identified on plan and that objective is to collect clues to help find treasure.

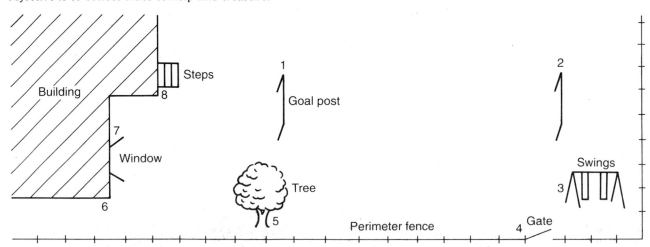

Development:
In pairs, pupils follow trail/plan, to collect card from each feature and arrange in order to find treasure.

Emphasise use of plan.
This can be made more difficult by removing the rope trail.

Conclusion:
Review activity with pupils.

136